Praise for *Secrets of Home Staging*

"I've had the privilege of mentoring Karen when she entered the home staging industry many years ago through my certification training at the Home Staging Resource. Having trained thousands of home stagers over the last fifteen years, I knew right away that Karen would be highly successful in this field. Karen has an innate ability to read a home, the home seller and communicate very clearly the 'whys' of home staging. Details matter when it comes to staging, so understanding the 'why' of decluttering, depersonalizing, and most importantly the 'styling' are the first steps in getting the best price for your most valuable commodity. *Secrets of Home Staging* is your how-to manual for breaking down the selling and staging process, so it feels less overwhelming and more doable... With Karen Prince's know-how in your hands, you got this."

　　—**Audra Slinkey**, president of the Home Staging Resource and the American Society of Home Stagers and Redesigners

"Karen Prince's *Secrets of Home Staging* is a must-read when selling your home. This book is a beautiful tutorial that will help you sell your home faster and for more money. If you follow Karen's advice, you will transform your space into every buyer's dream home."

　　—**Cassandra Aarssen**, professional organizer and author of *Real Life Organizing, Cluttered Mess to Organized Success Workbook, The Clutter Connection*, and *The Declutter Challenge*

"I love working with Karen! She really knows how to make a house appeal to buyers. Sellers are often skeptical of staging in general, but her professional and friendly manner puts them at ease. After the home is staged, they are often astounded by the transformation. Most importantly, they feel that the money spent on staging was well spent. Her staged homes show better and add value in the eyes of the buyer, buyer's agent, and the appraiser. I recommend her to all of my clients!"

—**Gina Cipriani LaPlaca**, licensed real estate salesperson

"Although skeptical, I hired Karen at the urging of my broker. When she completed the staging, I barely recognized my house—it was gorgeous! Most importantly, I received multiple offers and it sold for more than I expected. Karen did a terrific job and was a pleasure to work with. I even hired her to choose the paint colors for our new apartment."

—**Lynn Pagliaccio**

"She's simply the best—a true professional with the ability to meet deadlines and work within all types of budgets. Karen has a great eye and style, and her recommendations were spot on. All the realtors and house hunters mentioned that the house 'showed beautifully.' At one point after she worked her magic, I was VERY tempted to stay! I would highly recommend her for staging your home in advance of selling."

—**Emi Battaglia**

"Karen did an amazing job at advising us on how and what to declutter, choosing paint colors to enhance each room in our house, and making our home look its very best for selling. It was definitely a worthwhile investment of our time and money—our house sold quickly in a difficult market."

—**Mark Keefe**

"Karen's design and understanding of the market were key components in my house having six bids in seven days; we were in contract on the tenth day, and the final bid was well over asking."

—**Todd Matlovsky**

"Karen is a consummate professional who on our walkthrough pointed things out which we had never thought of... The day after the public open house we had five offers; within two days we had three more! Receiving and accepting an offer of almost 10 percent over the asking price is proof of the importance of staging, particularly with Karen."

—**Jeffrey O'Donnell**

Secrets of

Home
Staging

Secrets of
Home
Staging

The Essential Guide to
Getting Higher Offers...Faster!

Karen Prince

CORAL GABLES

Published by Mango Publishing Group, a division of Mango Media Inc.

Cover, Layout & Design: Karen Prince & Morgane Leoni
Cover Photo: © Trinette Reed/Stocksy / Adobe Stock
Interior Photos: All photos Adobe Stock except the following: Page 20: Lynne Reah; Page 46: Liz Pensiero; Pages 75(left), 76, 77, 81, 82, 84, 87, 90, 100, 150, 153, 156, 157, 158, 159, 160, 161, 162, 163, 169, 182, 184, 185, 186, 187, 189, 193, 194, 196, 199, 200, 202(top), 204, 205, 206, 207, 214(right), 229: Karen Prince; Page 75(right): Daniel Milstein Photography; Page 78: Jennifer Adams; Page 102: Peggy O'Connell; Page 123: Julie Wills; Page 197: Anne and Patrick Furlow; Page 214: Claire Cornish; Page 222: Anwesha Baner

For permission requests, please contact the publisher at:

Mango Publishing Group
2850 S Douglas Road, 2nd Floor
Coral Gables, FL 33134 USA
info@mango.bz

For special orders, quantity sales, course adoptions and corporate sales, please email the publisher at sales@mango.bz. For trade and wholesale sales, please contact Ingram Publisher Services at: customer.service@ingramcontent.com or +1.800.509.4887.

Secrets of Home Staging: The Essential Guide to Getting Higher Offers...Faster!

Library of Congress Cataloging-in-Publication number: 2021931765
ISBN: (p) 978-1-64250-554-2, (e) 978-1-64250-555-9
BISAC category code HOM011000, HOUSE & HOME / House Plans

Printed in the United States of America

Contents

Introduction

Buying a home is the largest investment most of us make, so when it comes to selling it, we have a *lot* riding on the success of that sale. The price we get for our home can affect where we live in the future, whether we can pay off debts, or whether we can afford to retire.

Home staging is a relatively recent marketing tool that has proven to be highly effective in selling homes faster and for a higher price. While I was running a home staging business, working daily with people preparing to put their homes on the market, universally, their number-one concern was whether they would get the price they wanted for their home. And since many were aware of the effect of home staging, they were very grateful for the help and information I was able to give them.

While there are many fantastic stagers out there to help home sellers—and I encourage you wholeheartedly to seek them out—I felt that most people would benefit from a book designed to guide them through the home staging process, packed with information and plenty of tips and tricks along the way. So that has been my goal. I've written this book for the average home seller who will probably be living in their home while it is on the market.

If that describes you, I've aimed to provide the information you need to ensure that your home shows well and that it appeals to buyers so that you get the best price possible. My hope is also to alleviate some of the stress of selling a home. With a plan in place, you'll feel better about getting your house ready and end up with a better result.

I have tried to make this book extremely practical so it can help real people with real houses, at a time when they can really use it. Home staging can be a ton of work and a huge inconvenience, so a lot of home sellers understandably resent the need to do it. Before listings were online, staging was something only wealthy people did, if anyone. Now it is done by almost every home seller—at least in part—and most everyone should consider doing more. Those who don't stage their home are at a huge disadvantage, selling alongside those who have.

For all the agents out there, this book is also for you. Being a real estate agent can be a tough (and sometimes thankless) job. This book should help you sell your listings faster and for more money. By helping your clients prepare their homes properly for sale, you will be providing them with good service and benefiting yourself as well. Occasionally, I found that some clients didn't understand why home staging was beneficial—often because they bought their current home before online listings existed—and were resistant to the idea. I hope this book helps those people, as well as the home sellers who are already sold on the idea of staging, but don't know where to start. And if you offer staging services as part of your package to home sellers, I hope this book gives you some fresh ideas that you had not thought of before.

This book is dedicated to the home sellers who inspired me to write it.

Home Staging Is a Powerful Selling Tool

Why Stage?

Home staging has become an increasingly important step in selling your home. When viewing properties online, prospective buyers make decisions in a matter of seconds, so first impressions really do matter! A homeowner has only a couple of seconds to engage a buyer before they swipe left and move on to the next listing.

There are a lot of practical considerations for buyers looking at a home: price, square footage, style, and location, location, location! These factors are important, but despite this, buyers will pass on many houses that meet their criteria. Why? Because buyers also have to make an emotional connection to a home before they will make an offer. This is, after all, not only the biggest investment most buyers will ever make, it is also the place where they might raise their family, work, spend most of their leisure time, and look forward to coming home to when they are away.

If they are to fall in love with your home and make a high offer, buyers need to envision themselves living happily within it. They will need to see themselves living an aspirational, idealized lifestyle in your living room, sleeping in your bedroom, and cooking in your kitchen—and they will need to imagine it as *their* new home, not yours. Home staging sells homes by helping buyers see past the current home sellers' belongings to imagine their own aspirational lifestyle. It "sets the stage" for them and paints a picture of a lifestyle that they want badly enough to pay top dollar for.

Why Home Staging Is *Not* the Same as Interior Design

Most people think that interior design and home staging are the same thing. But there are several differences and it's important to know them before you start your staging process.

First, the goal of the two is different. The goal of interior design is to create a home that appeals to a homeowner. The goal of home staging is to prepare a home to be sold at the highest price possible by appealing to as many people as possible. Interior design results in a home that is personal for the homeowners, using styles and colors that they love in ways that appeal to their own tastes and lifestyle. Home staging is a marketing tool that merchandises a home to appeal to the widest audience possible. Successful staging makes the home look great in marketing photos, highlights selling features, makes rooms feel large, and appeals to a broad market.

Did You Know?

97 percent of home buyers used the internet to search for homes.

Source: 2020 Profile of Home Buyers and Sellers, National Association of REALTORS®.

Second, money is allocated differently. With interior design, you want to spend money on quality items that will achieve a look that appeals to the homeowner and will function well according to the homeowner's lifestyle. With home staging, it is important to spend money only on things for which you will receive a high return on investment (ROI). Whether staging money is spent on updates, painting, repairs, or replacing furniture, it is spent with the intent of increasing the value of the home and the appeal of the home to potential buyers.

Finally, home staging results in a less crowded, less cluttered, and less personalized style than most people actually live with. Even the most beautifully designed and minimalist home can often use some simplifying, depersonalizing, and freshening up when preparing to go on the market.

The Importance of Online Photography and Videos

It can't be overstated how important online photography and videos are. Buyers will *only* go to see a home if they like how it looks online. They are generally very well informed about what is available in their market and will make a list of homes they want to see in their limited time. It is very difficult for a real estate agent to convince a buyer to view a home in person if the buyer has seen the online photos and already made their mind up that they're not interested.

You have about three seconds to make a good first impression online before you risk losing a lot of potential buyers. The key photo (usually of the front of a house) is the first one that needs to grab them. After that, the next three or four photos are the most important, because those are the photos that are going to create the strongest impression. Make sure those photos look great so that you've got the buyer wanting to scroll to see the rest of the photos and to add your home to their list of homes to visit. If you don't make it onto a high number of buyers' "favorites" lists, you will have fewer people come to see your home in person and, therefore, fewer potential offers.

Videos and online tours are also very important. Usually, if the photos look appealing, a prospective buyer will take the time to view a video or online tour. These tools give the buyers an even better sense of what the home is like. So they make it even more important that you spend some effort getting your home prepared for market. And they are even more important when buyers are not able to come see a home in person, such as during the Covid-19 pandemic or when a buyer lives out of the area.

There are several things you can do to make your home look great in online photography, which we will go through in Steps Four and Six.

Did You Know?

Buyers love 3D virtual tours because they allow them to preview just about every room from every angle. Will buyers like what they see of your home?

How to Attract Buyers

When staging your home, your number-one goal is to attract buyers. But how do you do that? It's easy! Here are the things that buyers *love*:

LIGHT AND BRIGHT

Try to make your home look as light and bright as possible. Dark and dingy rooms turn buyers off. Open all window treatments to their fullest (or simply take them down). Choose light colors over dark. Light, white spaces look better in online photos and feel more welcoming in person.

LARGE

Even small rooms can be made to look larger. Choosing the right furniture for each room and placing it correctly makes all the difference.

Buyers love light and bright homes that are well maintained and up to date.

CLEAN

A staged home should be absolutely spotless. Do the white glove test everywhere. Look up, look down, look around your home in places you normally don't think about. Buyers *love* clean homes and are very turned off by other people's dirt.

WELL MAINTAINED

A well-maintained home tells buyers that they won't have a lot of surprises and expenses when they move in. You will get a lot more interested buyers if your house feels like it has been taken care of. If buyers think your house has been neglected, they will drop their price—or go running.

UP TO DATE

Homes that are more in keeping with the latest interior design trends attract more buyers. It's likely that your home won't be the only one on the market in your price range. If buyers feel your home is fresh and current compared to the competition (especially if your target buyer is younger), they will be drawn to yours. When buyers see that a lot of updating needs to be done, they either lose interest in your home, or make a lower offer.

SELLING FEATURES

Be sure buyers notice your home's selling features. Make a list of yours! I've been in countless houses where wood-burning fireplaces have been obscured by large furniture. Know your home's selling features and be sure to showcase them. You might take for granted some things about your home, but you don't want buyers to.

Pro Tip!

"To prepare your home, take photos on your phone from each corner. Look at each photo and see what may appear awkward, sticks out, or is unclear. Remember, the way you live may not be the way your home shows best online."

Lynne Rhea
MomBo Interiors
Austin, TX
mombointeriors.com

Know Your Buyer

Okay, so now you know what generally appeals to buyers. But before you spend a dime or pick up a paint brush, it is important to determine your target audience. Who is your buyer likely to be? It is important to get into the mind of your prospective buyer in order to market your home to them.

Buyers in the market where this house is located love an eclectic mid-century modern look, so it was staged with this in mind. It sold immediately, 10 percent over list price. In other markets, this look might not have been as popular with buyers, so it is important to know who you are targeting.

Any successful product is marketed with a buyer in mind. Don't think of it as your own personal space anymore. Think of your home as a product for sale in a competitive market. Your home is probably your biggest investment, and you want to get the largest possible return on it.

The most successful home sellers are those who have detached emotionally from their home and think of it as a product that they have invested a lot of money in and would like to sell for the best possible price.

Talk to a real estate agent about potential buyers and what is important for them.

It's important to know your buyer because it's not about what you like or what you think is important in a home. What is essential to know is what your prospective buyers like and what they think is important in a home. Are they likely to be a family with small children? Show them where the kids will play by creating a play area if you don't already have one. Do they like white kitchen cabinets? Paint your kitchen cabinets! Who cares that you don't like white kitchen cabinets and don't have any small children? It's not about you. It's about marketing your home, which is now your "product," to the buyers.

Staging Tip!

Home sellers who stop thinking of their home as a reflection of themselves and their personal tastes—and start seeing their home as a product for sale—are the most successful.

Talk to your real estate agent and get a staging consultation to determine who your buyer is. These professionals can tell you what the buyer demographics are likely to be for your house based on your neighborhood, price point, style, and condition. Sometimes you may have a secondary buyer that you also want to target. In that case, target your main buyer primarily, but don't do anything that would turn away the secondary buyer. For instance, if your main target is young, first-time buyers and the secondary buyer is retirees who are downsizing you could still stage a bedroom as a children's bedroom because it would appeal to both young parents and grandparents who may have grandchildren visiting. But if there is a third bedroom, it could be styled as an on-trend guest room that would appeal to both buyers. A lot of first-time buyers will have guests to stay, most retirees will still respond to an on-trend look, and it is much better to err on the side of being current than old-fashioned.

Once you know your buyers, every decision you make about staging your home and getting it ready for market should be based on what your buyers are likely to be looking for.

Types of Home Staging Services Offered

Since home staging has become essential, the staging industry has expanded to fit every need of home sellers. Unless your home is a tear-down, there is probably a service that will benefit you. There are four main types of staging services offered. The right type for you is determined by your home itself, the home's price point, your time, and your budget.

STAGING CONSULTATIONS

In a staging consultation, a home stager will go through your home with a fresh and professional eye and will offer you invaluable advice. A good consultation should leave you with a prioritized plan and the information you need to make your home look its best.

Depending on the size of your home and the stager's style, consultations often take from one to three hours and usually cover a lot of recommendations, including:

- Furniture editing and placement
- Accessory editing and placement
- Repairs and updates
- Curb appeal
- Decluttering and depersonalization
- Deep cleaning
- Styling
- Possibly some paint recommendations

Some stagers will provide a written report, others suggest that you take your own notes during the consultation. A staging consultation is especially valuable if you plan on doing the staging yourself and don't plan to hire a stager to do any further staging services. But if you determine that you require the staging services listed below, you might decide to hire your consultant for further services after the consultation.

Many real estate agents pay for a staging consultation for their clients because they realize how valuable it can be in getting the best price. But if your agent doesn't offer this (or you don't have an agent lined up), pay for one yourself. It will be well worth the money. The stager should let you know the fee for the consultation before you schedule it. Keep in mind that a staging consultation is not the same as a quote. A quote is when a stager comes to your home solely with the intention of quoting a price for the staging services listed below and generally does not include the staging advice that would be offered in a consultation.

Staging consultations are recommended for all homeowners, no matter what your budget may be.

OCCUPIED STAGING

This is probably the most common type of professional home staging service after a consultation. "Occupied" simply means that a homeowner is living in the home while it is on the market. Since most people sell their current home before moving out of it, this is a very popular type of staging and can often be very cost effective.

Depending on your time and budget, a professional home stager may provide some rental furniture and accessories, painting services, decluttering, furniture rearranging, styling updates, and more. A lot of stagers will edit a homeowner's furniture and then add updated accessories which they will select for the homeowners. Sometimes the stagers will rent the accessories to the homeowner from their staging inventory, other times the accessories will be selected and purchased for the homeowner who will keep them after staging.

Home sellers are often amazed at the transformation that occupied staging can make—even when it uses all, or mostly all, their own belongings!

BEFORE

AFTER

Before and after photos of an occupied staging. In this living room, the walls were painted, the wall-to-wall carpet removed and fresh accessories added—resulting in an immediate sale!

VACANT STAGING

Vacant staging refers to staging empty homes, homes that are not occupied by anyone while they are live on the market. Unfurnished homes don't show as well online and take longer to sell than staged homes. Professional developers of new homes know this, which is why they have been spending a lot of money on staging model homes for decades. You can use the same principles that developers have been using for years to sell your own home.

Here are some reasons empty homes don't sell well.

1.   In online photos, without furniture as a reference, it's difficult to tell how big a room is and even what its purpose is. Is that a photo of the dining room or family room? Or is it a bedroom? It's hard to tell.

2.   Then, when buyers come to see a home, it's very difficult to tell how much furniture will fit in a space. Will this bedroom fit a king-size bed? Will a large sectional fit in the family room? You've lost the buyer at this point!

3. In homes with odd-shaped rooms, it's really hard for buyers to know how they can use the space. You need to show them by having furniture in the rooms. Don't make the mistake of assuming that buyers have imagination and vision, because most don't.

4. The main reason empty homes don't sell as well is that buyers can't connect emotionally to empty rooms. If that connection doesn't happen, buyers will move on.

If your home will be empty when you go on the market and you decide not to stage it, expect to receive fewer offers and for less money, than similarly sized staged homes in your market.

Whether you have a small or large budget, it is always to your advantage to stage your home rather than show it empty. If you won't be living in your home while it is on the market, you have several options on how to go about staging it. Before you move to your new place, perhaps you can select some of your furniture and accessories to leave behind for the staging. Then, once you've sold the house, you can move it to your new place.

BEFORE · AFTER

Before and after photos of a vacant staging. Adding furniture and accessories brings a room to life and increases its appeal.

But if that isn't an option, or if your home is in the luxury category, it can be well worth the cost to hire a professional home stager for a complete vacant staging. It is usually more expensive than occupied staging, since it requires more rental furniture and accessories, but the results are dramatic. It will result in a great transformation and the best possible response from buyers. A good professional home stager can change your home in ways you probably couldn't imagine. Homeowners sometimes think that the pricing of professional vacant staging is high, but that can easily be earned back in the form of a higher selling price and a quicker turnaround, meaning lower carrying costs and property tax payments.

VIRTUAL STAGING

Virtual staging is digital staging done for online and marketing purposes. Using photo editing software, furniture, rugs, artwork, and accessories are added to the photos of the home to show online buyers how the rooms could look. Sometimes paint colors are changed, repairs are completed, and even full renovations can be done. This type of staging is generally used for empty rooms or yards.

Virtual staging can help your home's appeal online, but buyers may be disappointed when they see it in person.

The benefit of virtual staging is that it is cheaper. It's a lot easier to put a digital couch in a room than a real couch. Plus, it doesn't have to be picked up afterward, so sellers save on both rental and moving costs. Another good thing about virtual staging is that, since the technology is pretty new, most of the furniture and accessories are fairly modern and on trend. If it is done well, it can look really good online and get buyers in the door.

The downside is that you can get the buyers' expectations up, and when they come to the home and see a house full of empty rooms, it can be a real letdown for them. Since there aren't any items of furniture or accessories to distract them, and if they're feeling disappointed, they are more likely to notice flaws they might otherwise have overlooked, and they are not likely to make a positive emotional connection with the home under these circumstances. However, if you've got empty rooms and a very small budget, at least it will help you get more people to come and see your home in person.

There are regulations against virtual staging in some areas, so before you decide to use virtual staging for your property, check your local regulations. Also, it is unethical to misrepresent your property, so be sure that you use this option wisely.

What Are Your Key Rooms?

Something that is useful to determine early on is, what are your key rooms? Key rooms are the rooms that have the biggest impact and are going to make or break your sale. These are the rooms that will have the biggest role in the buyer's decision-making process.

The key rooms in most homes are the kitchen, the primary bedroom (and en suite bath if there is one), and the rooms you see when you first walk in the door. So if you see the living room when you walk in, that is a key room. If you see a foyer, a living room, a dining room, and a second-floor landing, these are all key rooms. Also, if you see the corner of another room at the back of the house—maybe a portion of the family room down at the end of the hall from the front door—that corner is also a key space to pay attention to.

Why determine your key rooms before you start? Because these are the room you will focus on. It's smart to concentrate your time and money on your key rooms, since these are the rooms that have the most impact on the buyer's decision. And it makes your own decisions easy when you are faced with which rooms to paint, or whether it makes sense to purchase some updated accessories for a specific room. If it's in a key room, then yes, it's probably worthwhile. If it's not in a key room and your time or money is limited, you may be wiser to just clean and declutter that room, and otherwise leave it as is. Some home sellers on a budget hire a professional stager to stage the key rooms and then do the other areas of the home on their own.

Kitchens are almost always a key room to stage.

The Importance of Curb Appeal

If you've ever watched a home show on TV or know anything at all about real estate, you'll know that curb appeal is important.

The front of your home is the first thing buyers see, so you want to make sure you make a good first impression. Buyers will start forming an opinion about your home the moment they see it from their car. So your goal is to make buyers start falling in love with your home the first minute they get there.

After viewing online listings and making a list of the homes they are interested in, a lot of buyers will follow up with a drive-by. Especially if the buyers don't live too far away, they will drive slowly by (or walk by) your home to get a good look before deciding if they want to actually view it in person. If they don't like what they see when they drive by, they will cross your home off their list.

If you're selling an apartment, condominium, or co-op, you might not be able to do anything about the front of your building or your lobby, but you can make sure the door to your unit is clean, well maintained, and has a fresh doormat. If you've personalized your door with wreaths, flowers, a plaque with a cute saying, etc., now is the time to depersonalize. (See more about depersonalizing in Step Three.) Take down the plaque, and freshen up any dried flowers. Make sure that they're seasonal, but not specific to any holiday.

When to Call a Professional Home Stager

Every home on the market can benefit from a professional home stager in some way, even if you are working with a very tight budget. It doesn't need to cost you a lot. In fact, you shouldn't spend money on any staging services at all unless you are likely to earn your money back with a more successful sale. Here are just ten examples of when it makes sense to schedule an appointment with a home stager.

1. STAGING CONSULTATION

All homes going on the market need a staging consultation—every one. Consultations are usually between $250 and $700, which is nothing compared to the cost of a home, so that's a no-brainer. Definitely get a consultation.

2. PAINT COLOR CONSULTATION

If you need to do some painting before you go on the market, get a paint color consultation. There are literally thousands of paint colors to choose from, and picking the right one can be very tricky. Even white comes in enough shades and tints to confuse anyone without some training in color theory. A good professional home stager knows what colors appeal to buyers and will choose the best staging-friendly color for your home based on:

    a. the undertones of your flooring, cabinets, counters, and furnishings
    b. the light in each room
    c. any existing wall colors that will not be painted
    d. the style of your home

A consultation saves you a lot of time and money by getting the color right the first time and making your home look its best.

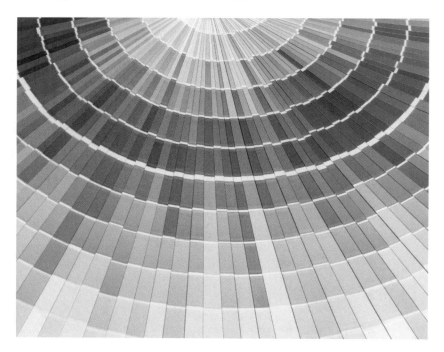

3. OCCUPIED STAGING

If you will be living in your home while it's on the market and aren't confident in your visual design sense or aren't up on the latest trends, hiring a home stager to work their magic will make a world of difference in the sale of your home.

4. UPDATING

Trends change every ten years. If your kitchen, bathrooms, furniture, and/or accessories are over ten years old, a stager can help you decide what and how to update in order to receive the best return on your investment.

5. FURNITURE EDITING AND PLACEMENT

If your furniture is large and your rooms are medium to small, your house is going to feel small and cramped. A stager can help you decide what to store while staging, how to arrange what you have, and possibly provide smaller-scaled rental furniture.

6. STAGING KEY ROOMS

Many homeowners hire a professional to stage the key rooms and do the remaining rooms themselves to keep on budget.

7. GOING UPSCALE

If you're in a pricey market, buyers' expectations are high, or the competition is fierce, and your home needs to kick it up a notch, a professional stager will transform your home so that you get top dollar.

8. NEED HELP?

If you're going through a hard time due to illness, death, divorce, bankruptcy, or other hardship, dealing with preparing your house for sale is probably more than you can take on. Moving is difficult in even the best of times. Stagers can take a lot off your plate and make the process much smoother and easier.

9. TIME CRUNCH

Is your time extremely limited? Do you need to get everything done quickly? Stagers will get it done for you.

10. VACANT STAGING

If your entire home or key rooms will be empty while it is on the market, a home stager will provide furniture and accessories that speak to buyers and increase your home's appeal dramatically.

Are Staging Services Worth Investing In?

Here are statistics from the Real Estate Staging Association (RESA)* 2020 survey of 13,000 staged homes:

1. ROI: With an average investment in staging services of 1 percent of the list price, approximately 75 percent of buyers saw an ROI of 5 to 15 percent over asking price.

2. Sales over listing price: 85 percent of staged homes sold for 5 to 23 percent over list price.

3. Average days on market: staged homes sell faster, averaging twenty-three days on market.

*   realestatestagingassociation.com.

What to Look for in a Professional Home Stager

So you want to talk to a stager. The first question you might have then is: How do you go about finding a good one?

If you're already working with a real estate agent, they probably have a relationship established with a favorite stager or two and will recommend that you work with them. This is usually a good way to go (assuming your agent is experienced in your market). After all, an agent's goal is to sell homes, so they make it their business to know the stagers who do a great job. You can also ask people you know or local groups on social media for recommendations.

When you are considering a particular stager, here are things to consider:

1. Check their portfolio to see their work—do they have before and after photos that show the level of service they provide? Can you see how their work would have added to the sale price of a home?

2. Do they have proper insurance?

3. Do they have professional training? While there are good stagers without professional home staging training, training in this field is helpful and indicates that you are working with a serious professional. Ask if they are a certified home stager.

4. Are they members of a professional staging organization? Again, there are good stagers who aren't a member of any organization, but those that are members are likely to be more professional and reliable. RESA is the official professional home staging trade organization and has been instrumental in establishing standard trade practice for home stagers worldwide. Its members agree to a code of conduct and professional standards and can be found at realestatestagingassociation.com.

5. Interview and get quotes from multiple stagers, and don't just go with the lowest bid. A quote that is significantly below others is a red flag that the stager isn't experienced or is underestimating the time and materials needed.

6. Search online to see reviews from a stager's previous clients. Most stagers are on houzz.com, so you can start by looking there. If a prospective stager doesn't have online reviews, ask for the contact info of some of their previous clients and contact them.

It pays to do a little homework before you commit to hiring a stager. I've been called to come to the rescue a number of times when the homeowner and real estate agent weren't happy with a job that a previous stager had done or was in the process of doing. Often the home seller had been trying to cut costs by hiring a less expensive and less experienced stager and ended up wasting money in the end by having the home staged twice—so do your homework before you hire someone!

Did You Know?

26 percent of home seller's agents personally offer staging services for their clients.

Source: 2019 Profile of Home Staging, National Association of REALTORS® Research Group.

Real Estate Agents Who Provide Staging Services

Agents know how valuable staging can be when it comes to selling a home. So, naturally, a lot of agents offer staging services. This can be a good thing—but only if the staging they provide is done well.

Agents can offer staging services in several ways.

REAL ESTATE AGENTS WHO DO THEIR OWN STAGING

Some agents physically do the staging themselves as part of their services for their clients. A lot of these agents do a fantastic job. They know their market and what buyers are looking for, and they have a great eye. But before you sign with an agent who is offering you this option, be sure you know that your agent is one of those who do a good job with the staging. Some do lackluster or even horrible jobs. Their staging is not worth anything if it's not done well, and you will be doing yourself a disservice if your home doesn't look its best. Ask to see photos of homes that they've staged and sold recently, and compare them to other listings in your market to make sure you are in good hands before committing.

REAL ESTATE AGENTS WHO OFFER STAGING DONE BY PROFESSIONAL STAGERS THROUGH THEIR BROKERAGE

A lot of agents will pay for staging services done by professional home stagers. Oftentimes an agent will pay for a staging consultation for their clients, and then any staging services required after the consultation are paid for by the homeowner. Sometimes agents or brokerages front the cost of all the staging needed and it is considered part of their concierge services. Then the homeowner usually pays the costs back when they close on the home. Again, be sure you know ahead of time if the stagers they hire are going to do a good job. You should still consider the same factors when committing to a staging service, no matter what your arrangement is with your agent.

Summary

- Home staging is a marketing tool used to merchandise a home so that it appeals to the widest audience possible.

- Home staging will help your home get on buyers' must-see lists with great online photos.

- Home staging helps buyers imagine themselves living the life they dream about and allows them to make an emotional connection to a home—which translates into an offer.

- Buyers love homes that are light, bright, well maintained, move in ready, clean, uncluttered, and up to date.

- Determine your target buyer and then make your staging decisions based on what your buyers are looking for.

- Determine your key rooms so that you spend your staging dollars wisely.

- Depending on your home, your home's price point, your time, and your budget, there is a staging service that can help you achieve top dollar.

Before You Start

The Six Steps to Successful Staging

There are six basic tasks that you will want to consider when staging your home. Each of these tasks will be covered in detail in the following chapters, but it's good to have an overview of what you would like to achieve so that you have a rough idea of the scope of your own staging project.

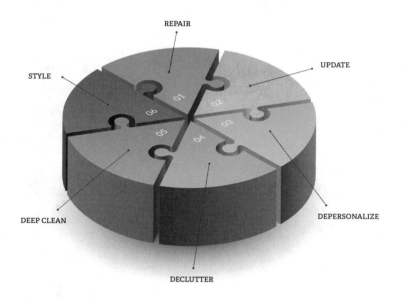

These six steps can be applied to any room, including your storage spaces and the garage, and they also can be applied to the exterior of your home, which will increase your curb appeal.

They can be done in any order, but I recommend that you start by addressing your repairs and updates. Repairs and updates often take the longest to get done since they often involve getting quotes, budgeting, inspections, and permits. You can often be at the mercy of your local tradespeople's schedules, which are invariably not as convenient as a homeowner wants them to be. So it's best to start with the repairs and updates.

When to Start

The sooner you have a staging plan, the better. It's better to do a little each week than to procrastinate and panic right before you go on the market. Moving is stressful, even in the best circumstances. It's even more stressful if you leave things till the last minute.

If you have been in your home ten years or longer, I recommend starting a *full year* before you plan on going on the market—if possible. There are three reasons for this:

1. You've probably accumulated a lot, and it will take longer than you think to go through everything, sort it, and find homes for the items that you are going to donate or sell. If you have raised children in the home, you probably have a lot of toys and clothes that they have long outgrown. Decluttering will take some time.

2. There are also probably a lot of repairs and painting needed that you're comfortable living with and probably don't even notice anymore, but would need to be fixed before you go on the market and will require some budgeting consideration.

3. The longer you've lived in a home, the more updates are necessary, since you probably made a lot of design decisions such as paint colors and window coverings that are now outdated and will be a turnoff for buyers.

If you've been in your home only a short time and you don't have a lot of things, a month or so might be enough. But for those who have been in their homes for many years, there will be a lot more to do.

Schedule Your Staging Steps

You may be dying to get started on staging your house immediately, but it's so important to plan first! You'll save yourself a lot of time, money, and energy if you start with a plan. You don't want to waste time doing things that aren't necessary—you want to be sure that the things that you do are worthwhile and will actually help the sale of your house. Don't get sidetracked. Concentrate on only doing tasks that will actually help the sale of your house.

So the first step is to create your plan. But if you are really, really dying to start before having a full plan in place, and you know that you have a lot of decluttering ahead of you, I recommend that you do a *little* bit of decluttering each day while reading this book and creating your plan. Spend a *maximum* of fifteen minutes a day doing the decluttering until you have a *full plan* for your staging. You need to focus most of your energy on finishing this book and *getting a plan in place*.

Keep a Staging Journal

Keeping a staging journal can help you stay organized throughout your home preparation process.

I recommend that you start keeping a staging journal right at the beginning. There are a lot of things to keep track of, and keeping everything in one place will help you be organized and will relieve some stress. It can be a paper journal or a digital spreadsheet, it doesn't matter—whichever you feel most comfortable with. But please don't go and buy a new app or a special pretty paper journal! Any old school notebook, repurposed binder, Excel or Word doc, Google doc, or whatever organizing system you are already comfortable with is best. You don't want to put your energy into the journal itself or spend time on making it perfect and pretty. You want to put your energy into making your *house* look perfect and pretty. Just make sure your journal is practical for you and fits your preferred style of working.

Since there are other aspects involved in selling your home besides staging, you may find it helpful to expand the scope of your journal so it also includes any other information pertaining to the sale of your house. Here is a list of things you may want to keep track of in your journal. These entries will vary a lot, depending on your home, the market expectations in your area, your time, and your budget.

- Your target buyer (see page 21)
- Your key rooms (see page 28)
- Staging consultation notes (see page 23)
- A list of the rooms in your home with the following info:
  - Paint color recommendations (see page 87)
  - Repairs needed (see page 47)
  - Updates planned (see page 46)
  - Furniture to be removed (see page 162)
  - Curb appeal plan (see page 30)
- Quotes for repairs, updates, landscaping, professional staging

- List of items to sell
- List of items to donate
- Charities to donate to
- Storage unit info
- Schedule
- Budget
- Real estate agent information
- Comps (comparable properties in your neighborhood that are similar in size and condition)
- Deed and title information
- Lawyer/notary information
- Survey
- Permits required

About Planning

Often the list of tasks lying ahead of a home seller can feel overwhelming and almost infinite. If this is how you feel, please know that this is true of pretty much every homeowner attempting to get their home ready for the market. I've met with hundreds of homeowners, and I don't think I ever met with anyone who wasn't at least a little stressed-out about it. And most people are a lot more than a little stressed.

The upside of staging is that it really helps sell your home. The downside is that it can be a whole lot of work and create a lot of pressure on home sellers.

If you have a high-end home and a healthy budget for staging, you can hire a stager to do most everything—and you will likely get that money back in the sale of your home. If that's your situation, I highly recommend it. A professional home stager can transform your home in ways that you will probably not imagine.

But if you will be playing a large role in the staging of your home, this book is designed to help you. By the time you get to the end, you will know how to review the repairs and updates needed for your home and create a plan, a schedule, and a budget. You will know to depersonalize your home quickly. You will create a schedule and a plan for decluttering and deep cleaning. You will improve your home's curb appeal. And you will learn how to style your home so it looks its best.

Deciding Not to Stage

Whether you do it yourself or hire a professional stager, this book will help you with the process. However, if you're just not able to do any of the suggestions in this book for whatever reason, please don't worry about it. There is a buyer for every home. Your selling price or time on market will likely be negatively affected if you put your house up for sale with zero preparation, but it's a lot simpler, and maybe that's what you need to do. Every home seller has a unique situation that they are dealing with. Accept your situation, do what's right for you, and move on.

Plan Your Repairs and Updates

For most people, the idea of home staging conjures up images of hanging artwork, plumping up pillows, and adding vases filled with fresh flowers. These are all things you may want to do when staging your home, but in fact, the term "home staging" goes much deeper than that and generally encompasses everything you may

Money-Saving Tip!

Doing your own repairs and updates can pay off with a higher return on your investment and increase your home equity.

need to do to your home before you put it on the market. And a lot of these tasks are much more important to increasing the value of your home than those in which throw pillows are used.

So, while this book will give you lots of tips about styling with throw pillows, artwork, plants, and other fun things, there are two things you should prioritize over styling: repairs and updates. Later we will cover decluttering, depersonalizing, and cleaning, which are also very important—and mostly free!

Why Do Repairs?

You may not immediately think of repairs as being part of the staging process, but in fact, doing needed repairs is crucial to getting the best price for your house. When stagers and real estate agents make recommendations to homeowners who are considering putting their home on the market, repairs are often the first issue they address. You don't want to overlook this step, because many potential buyers will be turned off by homes where repairs have gone undone. Remember, buyers are most attracted to properties that feel well maintained and are move in ready. Doing needed repairs will boost your number of seriously interested buyers.

Most homeowners have a number of repairs that they have been putting off. If you're going to put your house on the market, now is the time to make them a priority.

Pro Tip!

*"Buyers will have a hard time evaluating a property if they are distracted by the color on the walls. We live in our homes very differently than how we sell them, therefore make sure any taste-specific colors are changed out for softer, more neutral tones that almost disappear and appeal to a wider market, allowing the structure of the home to shine through. There is no more impactful transformation **or** higher return on your investment than a gallon of paint!"*

Liz Pensiero
Liz Pensiero Staging
& Designs
Stamford, CT
lizpensierostagingdesigns.com

What Are Updates and Why Would I Do Them?

Updates are when you replace things in your home that have become outdated. They may still work and may have been all the rage at one point, but now these things will just turn buyers off. If you've been living in your home more than ten years, buyers' tastes have changed since you moved in, and there are probably simple updates you can do to help your home appeal to today's buyer. Remember that, to get the best price for your home, you want to appeal to buyers. The longer you have been living in your home, the more important it is to do some updates.

Also, if your target buyer is significantly younger than you are, updating some things in your home to appeal to these buyers can be very beneficial. Remember that, before a buyer can make an offer, they have to be able to envision themselves living in a home and love that vision. It's hard for them to do that when they're staring at a lot of outdated items or features that make them feel like they're in a parent's or grandparent's home.

You might say, "Let the new owners do the updates. They can decide what they like and do it themselves." If you did, you'd be assuming that buyers aren't impacted by what they see (they are), that they can visualize something other than what is in front of them (most can't), that they would prefer to do the updates themselves (they don't), and that they have the time to do them (most don't). By doing updates before you sell, you drastically expand the number of your potential buyers to include all normal, busy people, rather than restricting it to people who have the ability to visualize beyond what they see and have the time and energy to take on projects. And of course, more potential buyers means more potential offers!

List Your Repairs and Updates

Since repairs and updates can take a while to complete, they're one of the first things that you'll want to take stock of when you're planning to sell your home. It's important that you be organized about what needs to get done at the beginning. You don't want to have a plumber in to fix a sink one day, only to realize a week later that you should have asked him or her to fix a leaky pipe in the garage at the same time.

First, I recommend that you get your staging journal and go from room to room in your house. Make a list of the repairs and updates needed in each room until you have a list for the whole house. At this point, just put down every issue you see. Don't worry about prioritizing, just put down every possible repair and update.

Key Point!

Completing repairs before your house goes on the market is crucial to getting your best price.

It's difficult to be objective about your own home, so in order to help you with this, I have outlined the most common repairs and updates that all home sellers should consider in Steps Four, Five, and Six. Refer to these chapters as you make your own list. They should help you notice repairs that you might have otherwise overlooked and updates that will boost the appeal of your home.

Make sure you review the outside of your home as well as the basement, garage, and any storage areas.

Prioritize Your To-Do List

Once you have your unedited list, you need to determine the priority items and concentrate on doing only the prioritized tasks. Know that you don't need to do every single one of the many things on your list. If you only get a few priority tasks done, you will have increased the appeal of your house. So be proud that you have done those things and go to market. But the more the better, so if you're able to get a lot of items checked off your list, even better!

So how do you determine your priorities?

There are certain repairs that are pretty much essential (unless you are selling your house "as is," in which case no repairs or staging will be done), and other issues that are nice to get to if you have time. The most important repairs are the ones that are red flags for buyers. These are the most important tasks for you to take care of before you go on the market, since each one is a signal that there are large problems to be dealt with and will turn off a large segment of buyers. Updates can increase the appeal and value of your home and therefore should be considered at the same time, since they are often done simultaneously with the repairs.

1. RED FLAGS

Some examples of red flags are: water damage and saggy ceilings (could signal mold, leaky roof, or other recurring water issues); cracks in ceilings, walls, or foundation (could signal structural issues); sloping or cracked floors (more structural issues); termites or other insect and rodent issues; odors; standing water outside. If you have a whole lot of these issues, you might do best to sell your house as is, in which case staging is not necessary. Speak to your real estate agent about it. But if your home is generally in good shape but has a hint of any of these issues, you should prioritize fixing them. When you do fix them, try to finish the job so there is no sign of the repair. For instance, if there is a water spot on the ceiling from when your upstairs toilet overflowed three years ago and the toilet was fixed a long time ago, be sure you paint the whole ceiling, not just where the water spot is. If a potential buyer sees that only a portion of the ceiling was painted, they will suspect there was an issue. You don't want to bring doubt unnecessarily to your potential homeowners.

Of course, if there are actual issues such as those listed above, it is your obligation to either fix them or, if you don't fix them, not hide them. Your goal is not to deceive your buyers. Your goal is simply to present your home in its best possible light and let the buyers make an informed decision.

Water damage is a red flag to buyers, so first correct the problem and then remove traces of it before you put your home on the market.

2. KEY ROOMS

The to-do items in your key rooms need to take priority over those in other rooms. (See page 28 about determining your key rooms.) If you prioritize the repairs and updating to be done in your key rooms, they will have a greater positive impact on your sale.

3. BUDGET

Updates that are free or cheap and will have a big impact should be prioritized over those that are pricey or will not likely be important to buyers. You need to find out the costs involved to see which ones give you the most bang for your buck. So get quotes from professionals where applicable, and figure your time and materials for the repairs you'll do yourself.

4. WHAT'S IMPORTANT TO YOUR POTENTIAL BUYERS?

Speak to your real estate agent and your stager during the staging consultation and get their opinions on which changes are most important to buyers.

5. TIME

How much time do you have? If an update will take six months to complete and you want to be on the market in three months, cross that one off your list. When you have your list narrowed down, the to-do items that can be completed quickest should be prioritized. Get them done first and cross them off your list. Then, if you have more time, move on to the tasks that take a little longer. You'll feel better knowing that you've got some things done, and you'll be able to notice the difference yourself right away. This will also help you stay more motivated and make it easier to tackle the more difficult tasks.

Action Your List

Once you've prioritized your to-do list, it will be more manageable. Now it's time to plan how and when the list will get done.

Beside each entry on your list, indicate who will make the repair, whether it is yourself, a family member, friend, or professional. For instance, on your master list, you may list painting, and then under painting, you could list each room that needs some painting done and what needs to be done in each of the rooms. Beside each entry, you can say whether you will be doing that part of the painting yourself or hiring someone. If you will need a professional, indicate what type of pro you will need. For instance, if the hall bathroom sink is leaky and you're not able to fix it, under "Hall Bath" write, *leaky sink: plumber.*

Time to Schedule

Estimate how long the repairs are going to take and then double that. Everything always takes longer than you think. Once you have quotes from your professionals, get them started as quickly as you are able to. And for the repairs you will be doing yourself, add them all to your calendar and make sure you stay on top of them. If you're not able to keep up with your plans, adjust your calendar or enlist the help of friends, family, or professionals to get the jobs done.

Staging Tip!

Make it a priority to get quotes from tradespeople and get on their schedules as soon as possible.

Fine-Tune for Maximum Buyer Appeal

When you know which repairs and updates you are going to do, make sure you plan how you are going to do them with the buyer in mind. For instance, if you need to do some painting, be sure your new paint colors will appeal to buyers. Read about paint colors (page 87) or hire a professional for a paint color consultation. If you are going to replace some outdated light fixtures or bathroom fixtures, be sure to choose ones that appeal to your buyer. A stager can help you with your selection if you're not sure about it.

Get Started!

Don't delay on contacting any tradespeople to get quotes and get on their schedules. Start the projects that you will be tackling. Get friends and family lined up if they will be pitching in. The sooner you get this work done, the better. If all goes well, you may even be able to live with your new and improved home for a while and enjoy it!

Summary

- The six steps to successful staging can be applied to any room in the house and can also be used to boost your curb appeal.

- Use a staging journal to stay organized.

- Start the preparation for your home sale as soon as possible.

- Plan first before you start. This will save you a lot of headache, stress, time, and money.

- Making key repairs and updates is important to the sale of your home.

- Repairs and updates are the first thing you should take stock of when you're preparing your home for the market, since they can take a while to complete.

- First make a complete list of repairs and updates to consider, and then prioritize that list.

- Determine who will do each of the tasks (get quotes if applicable).

- Create a schedule.

- Plan your styles and colors (preferably in consultation with your real estate agent or local home stager).

- Get started!

Step One: Repairs That Sell Your Home

This chapter outlines common repairs that are needed for a lot of homes. You may question the need for reading over a list of repairs, but having done hundreds of staging consultations, I find it is helpful for almost all homeowners to have someone point these things out. It is extremely common to become blind to the everyday imperfections that we live with after living in a home for a while. By reading through these lists, you may find some important fixes that you want to take care of.

Exterior: Front, Back, and Sides

Curb appeal is always important. So with that in mind, here are some of the repairs you should look at before you put your home on the market. If any of these are required for your home, put them on your "Repairs and Updates" list.

1. Front walk. If you have a front walk, be sure that it is clean, safe, and in good repair. Are the stones uneven or crumbling? Or are there weeds poking up between them?

2. Driveway. Does your driveway need resurfacing? Maybe it's time to fill in some potholes and reseal. Or perhaps you have cracks on the concrete or need to replace some damaged stonework.

3. Steps. Repair or paint as necessary. Of course you want to make sure they are safe, but also, buyers' eyes will be on them when they walk up to your front door. So be sure that the paint or stain is fresh (if they are wood), or that the concrete, stone, or other materials are in good repair.

4. Shutters and gutters. Paint or repair if necessary.

5. Porch, patio, or deck. View these features with a critical eye and add any needed repairs to your list. Are they up to code and safe?

6. Siding or brick exterior of home. If your home has wood siding, you want to make sure that the paint is fresh-looking. If not, start getting quotes on getting it repainted. Brick homes tend to need less maintenance, but if there are cracks or repairs needed, make sure that you attend to them.

7. Power-wash. Power-wash the exterior of your home shortly before you go on the market.

8. Pool and hot tub. If you have a pool or other recreational features, you want to make sure they are a selling point, not a detriment to selling. Having them in good repair will help ensure this.

9. Garage. Be sure that the door is in working order and that your garage appears well maintained.

10. Sheds and play structures. If these are in good shape and don't crowd your outdoor space, then it is a good idea to keep them while showing. If they are in bad repair, or placed in a way that makes your yard appear smaller, take them down.

Front Door Area

Buyers may be standing for a few minutes outside your home while their agent deals with keys or lock boxes. While they're waiting for the agent to let them in, they'll be looking around and forming an opinion, so you want to make sure that the front door itself and everything in that immediate area are in good shape.

Here are some commonly needed repairs. Check to see any of them apply to you, and if they do, add them to your list.

Staging Tip!

Start outside when making your repairs list, because this is where buyers will make their first impression. View every feature of your house and property with a critical eye and add the needed repairs to your list.

1. Doorbell. Make sure your doorbell works and that the button is not cracked or discolored.

2. Door. Does your door open and close easily without squeaking? Does it have cracks that need filling, painting, or staining?

3. Screen door. Do you have an old screen door that has seen better days? Either replace it or take it off completely. They are nice to have when you're living in a house, but they don't add any benefit when selling. So if they are a little shabby, I recommend removing them. Houses often look better from the street without them.

4. Door sill. These are often worn and need staining, painting, or replacing.

5. Outdoor lights. Make sure they are clean and in good repair, and that the light bulbs are functioning and appropriate for the fixtures.

6. Door frame. Check to see if it needs any repair or touch-ups.

7. Door hardware. Does the finish of your door handle match the lock, the door knocker, mailbox, house number, or any other hardware features that you may have near your doors? Do any of them need to be replaced?

8. Porch, soffits, railings. Stand outside your front door for several minutes and have a serious look at everything. Make note of anything that needs attention.

9. Inside your front door. Have a good look at the inside of your front door and make note of any repairs, painting, or staining that need to be done.

Buyers may have to stand at your front door waiting while their real estate agent deals with the lock. So make sure they have something pleasant to look at while they stand there. You don't want to make a bad impression before they even walk into the house!

Floors

Floors are key to the visual impact of your home. Remember to keep the buyer's perspective in mind when you are considering repairs to your floors.

WOOD FLOORS:

If you already have exposed hardwood floors, then you're lucky. Replace any damaged sections. If the floors are scratched or very worn looking, you should sand and polyurethane them. If they're not in bad shape, try using a floor luster product (such as Quick Shine) designed for wood floors. This can save a lot of money and hassle and your floors will look great in online photos.

Money-Saving Tip!

Wood floors can often be revitalized by using a floor luster product. You may be able to save money by avoiding a sanding and polyurethaning project.

WALL-TO-WALL CARPET:

Wall-to-wall carpet is (at the time I am writing this) out of trend and, in most cases, turns buyers off. If you have wood floors underneath wall-to-wall carpet, definitely remove the carpet and show the wood floors.

If you don't have wood floors under your carpet, but your carpet is in good shape, make sure that it is clean. In key rooms of homes at higher price points, you should consider removing the carpet and adding hardwood floors. Get some quotes and talk to your real estate agent or local stager to help determine if it is worth the investment. Many of the homeowners I have worked with have done this with and been very happy that they did. Depending on your home's price point, you may want to consider engineered hardwood, which is more affordable than traditional hardwood.

Repair Tip!

Squeaky floors can often be quieted with baby powder. Just shake some down between the floorboards and, if possible, use a small brush to push the powder around. The powder can ease the friction and therefore stop the squeaking.

TILE FLOORS:

Be sure that your tile floors are in good shape, especially if they are in key rooms. If you are able to replace cracked tiles with matching tiles, then do that. Make sure your grout is in good shape and clean. If your grout looks dirty and you're not sure how best to clean it effectively, go online to determine which treatment is right for you. There are many videos on YouTube showing solutions for cleaning grout. Cleaning the grout on a floor can make an amazing difference.

LAMINATE AND VINYL FLOORS:

Laminate and vinyl flooring have come a long way. High-quality flooring created with various synthetic products is available in sheets, tiles, and wood-like planks. If your existing flooring is worn, replace it with new laminate or vinyl flooring in an on-trend style or color. It's a great way to give your room a facelift.

OTHER TYPES OF FLOORING:

Bamboo, cork, stone, linoleum, rubber, carpet tiles, concrete, and other poured materials are just some of the many other popular types of flooring available. Whichever type of floors you have, be sure they are well maintained and clean for maximum buyer appeal.

The Secret to Repairs that Sell Your Home: Start Early

Knowing how long a repair is going to take is almost impossible. It's very rare that a home repair goes completely smoothly, without any complications, on schedule—and starting one repair often leads to another. If you are hiring a handyman or contractor to do the work, you're at the mercy of their schedule and other jobs they are working on. If you're doing the repairs yourself, you will at least have more control over the scheduling, but most repairs take longer than you think, and you'll still need to factor in extra trips to the hardware store and more hours on YouTube when unforeseen issues invariably pop up. So, if you don't want to delay your home's listing, start early! The worst that can happen is that you get your repairs done ahead of schedule and enjoy them yourself.

Walls, Trim, Doors, and Ceilings

WALLS AND CEILINGS:

If you have any cracks in your walls or ceiling, you'll definitely want to patch them so that buyers don't have any questions about the structural integrity of your home. If you are considering painting only part of a wall or only part of your ceiling to save time or paint, think again. You'll probably end up making it look worse if you do this. Paint the whole ceiling or wall. *And definitely consider new paint colors!*

Don't just use the same paint as you had previously. Choosing the right paint colors is very important to the appeal of your house. It is *so* important to use staging-friendly colors! For help in choosing the right color, read Step Two, page 87 or book a local stager for a color consultation.

DOORS AND TRIM:

Be sure that all doors open and close properly. Sliding doors often have problems with the tracks and hinged doors often need hinges tightened or adjusted. Also check the trim around the doors and throughout the house to see if there are any damaged parts that need fixing. Make a note of needed paint touch-ups.

Lighting

Repair and replace any broken light switches. Replace burned-out light bulbs using the correct bulbs for that fixture. If hardwired lights aren't working, have the wiring repaired.

Windows

Replace any broken or cracked glass. Be sure that your windows slide open and closed easily. Replace weather stripping if necessary. Repair or replace any broken shades that will be staying on the windows while you are on the market.

Kitchens

The kitchen is always a key room, so make sure everything in your kitchen is in good repair. Here are some things to look for:

CABINETS:

1. Test the drawers to make sure that they slide easily.

2. Open and close the cabinet doors and tighten any loose hinges and handles.

Repair Tip!

Buyers love a well-lit home, so repairing any lighting issues is a good staging investment.

3. The cabinets below the sink are often the most worn. It's a high-traffic zone and, with all that water is nearby, the cabinet fronts take a beating, so repair any water damage that has happened to the base cabinet frames and doors.

4. Have a look at the cabinets around the stove and other places that might have been affected by heat—such as near the toaster or above a kettle. Be sure to repair damage to the cabinet wood or veneer.

5. Note paint touch-ups needed.

6. If your cabinet knobs and drawer pulls are worn or damaged, consider buying new ones. This is also a good idea if your knobs are outdated because of the finish or style, since it is a quick and easy update that you can do for very little money. It is a cheap fix and can improve the appearance of your cabinets.

7. Prospective buyers will look inside your cabinets, so before they do, have a close and careful look yourself and make a list of items that need fixing. Check inside all of the cabinets, especially under the sink. Do they look brand-new, clean, and well maintained? If not, give them a scrub and possibly a coat of paint and some shelf liner.

APPLIANCES:

If you need to repair appliances, put that on your list. If the repair is pricey, then it might be worth your while to replace instead. Speak to your real estate agent, especially before buying big-ticket items. Depending on the price of your home and your market you might be better off leaving them as is.

Repair Tip!

Before you start repairs, make a list of those you need to consider, get pricing, and prioritize which ones are most crucial to the sale of your home.

BACKSPLASH:

If your backsplash is looking shabby or is very dated, consider replacing it with neutral ceramic, marble, or encaustic tiles, preferably in white or cream to brighten up the space. If that's out of your price range, there are other budget-friendly alternatives. Vinyl adhesives can be applied over drywall or flat tiles for a nice clean look. Ceramic tiles can be reglazed. Beadboard backsplashes add farmhouse charm. And peel-and-stick faux tiles can be a great alternative as well.

SINK:

Be sure that the faucet is working well and isn't loose. Replace worn caulking.

TILES:

Replace any broken tiles.

Bathrooms

Bathroom repairs are almost always worth doing. If your bathroom is very outdated and you won't be updating it, at least be sure that any repairs are done and that the room is very clean. Your goal should be for buyers to come away thinking that they would like to renovate it at some point, but that they don't need to do it before they move in.

Repair Tip!

To apply caulk smoothly, have a cup of water handy. After applying the caulk with your caulking gun, simply dip your finger in the water and run it along the caulk to create a nice smooth line.

GROUT AND CAULKING:

Be sure that all grout and caulking is new-looking and clean. This is an easy, inexpensive repair that is always a good idea, since old and dirty-looking grout and caulking can be a real turnoff. Replacing crumbling or discolored caulking is one of the most common and easiest repairs needed before going on the market.

MEDICINE CABINETS:

Medicine cabinets that are in disrepair are often not worth replacing. They are not so much on trend now, and it is difficult to get the same size anyway. It is better to take out the cabinet, patch and paint the wall, and replace the cabinet with a large mirror.

VANITY, SINK, AND FAUCET:

Be sure that these are all in good repair, paint touch-ups are done, and everything works well. If not, before you replace anything, see the section in the next chapter on updating bathrooms.

SHOWER DOORS:

Be sure that they are functioning and in good repair.

LIGHTING:

Lighting is always important. Remember, light and bright! Make sure that all light fixtures are functioning and have working light bulbs.

Repair Tip!

Ever have a light bulb break in the socket and wonder how to get it out? First, cut a potato in half, turn off the power, and put on some safety gloves. Then push the cut side of the potato into the broken bulb and turn to the left—the bulb should come right out.

TUB AND SHOWER SURROUNDS:

Check caulking and grout. Remove shower caddies.

TOILETS:

Be sure toilets are in good working order. Replace the toilet seat if it is at all damaged or discolored. Replace toilet if it is damaged or old. When in doubt, a new clean white toilet is never a bad idea.

WALLS AND CEILING:

Patch and paint where necessary, using stager-friendly colors.

FAN:

A lot of old exhaust fans are noisy and can be a turnoff. New fans are not very expensive and are so much quieter. Sometimes changing to a quieter fan can transform the atmosphere of a bathroom and make it feel much more tranquil and inviting.

Five Reasons to Do a Pre-Inspection

What is a pre-inspection? A pre-inspection is an inspection done by a qualified home inspector, paid for by the home seller and conducted before a home is listed. As a home seller, why would you consider spending money on a pre-inspection?

1. You'll be aware of all repairs that may be needed and not be blindsided by unforeseen issues when the buyer's inspection is done.

2. You'll have a list of repairs to consider and prioritize.

3. You'll have control as to how you do the repairs and which contractor you use—if something comes up in the buyer's inspection report, you may not have that option.

4. You'll be able to use pricey upgrades in your home's selling copy: a new electrical panel, a new roof, a new furnace, will help sell your home.

5. You'll avoid negotiations after the sale and lower your stress.

If your home is new or recently renovated, you probably don't need to do one, but if your home is older or you have specific concerns, it might be money well-spent. Talk to your real estate agent since every home is different and laws concerning disclosing information differs as well.

Water Damage

Water Damage is *so* important to take care of. If a potential buyer sees signs of water damage, it is an immediate red flag. Water problems are often long-term and very expensive to deal with, and they make a buyer wary.

Since most water problems are inherently urgent and get taken care of right away, you may have already addressed your water problems. For instance, if you had a burst pipe, you would have immediately had it fixed. But often the damage done by a burst pipe is not immediately addressed. Ceilings often have water marks from old leaks in second-floor bathrooms. If that's the case, paint the entire ceiling. You don't want buyers to question the soundness of your plumbing. If you have damaged drywall, replace it now.

If you suspect mold might be an issue for your house, arrange a test for mold yourself before you go on the market. It is often cheaper and simpler to address a mold problem yourself without involving the buyer, their inspector, and their real estate agent in the mold remediation. Checking for issues that you may not know exist will allow you to avoid surprise fixes before they are discovered by the buyer's inspector and will save you money and time in the long run.

If you have any long-standing water related problems, you should take care of them before you go on the market. If they are going to come up in the inspection, you usually save money by addressing the problem beforehand. If the inspector finds it, the price of the repair may be estimated and deducted from your sale price. And the estimation is likely to be higher than you would actually pay. So take care of this first.

Repair Tip!

If you're not experienced at dealing with mold issues, make your health a priority and hire a pro.

Often, it makes sense to have an inspector come to your house before you sell it to raise any red flags that may come up. That way you have time to address the problems on your own terms before you sell the house.

Pest Control

I think it goes without saying that pests such as rodents and insects are *huge* buyer turnoffs. But the truth is, they are in almost every home at some point—and some more than others. If you have unaddressed issues with either insects (especially ones that cause structural damage, such as termites or carpenter ants) or rodents (which can also cause structural damage, disease, and fire hazards), get that taken care of and make it a priority!

Summary

- Completing outdoor repairs boosts your curb appeal.

- Check your front door area for repairs. Buyers may be standing there for a few minutes while their agent deals with the lock box.

- Floors are key to the visual impact of your home.

- Before you patch and paint your walls, be sure that you're using staging-friendly colors.

- Your kitchen is a key room, so make sure that everything in that room is in good repair.

- Bathroom repairs are essential to a successful sale.

- Make it a priority to fix any red-flag issues before you put your home on the market.

Step Two: Updates Buyers Love

The longer you have been living in your home, the more important it is to update. Buyers' tastes have probably changed since you moved in, and remember: the more you can do to appeal to prospective buyers, the better. Buyers will pick up on these updates when they view your photos online and be more likely to want to see your home in person—and the more people come to see your house, the more likely you are to get multiple offers.

Kitchen Updates That Sell

Kitchens are almost always a key room, so money spent carefully on kitchen updates is money well-spent! Generally, kitchen design trends change about every ten years. If your kitchen is older than that, there is a good chance that it is outdated.

If you're not sure if your kitchen is considered outdated or you're not sure what the latest kitchen trends are, do a little research online and on social media for latest trends in kitchens. Pay attention to the styles that are the most common, light, and neutral. Then start thinking about what you can do in your kitchen to achieve the look you're seeing. Or better yet, have a staging consultation and ask your stager. It's their job to keep up with the latest trends and to know what buyers are looking for in their area.

COMMON KITCHEN UPDATES

1. Change the color scheme: walls, accents, and accessories.
2. Change the cabinet color: painting or changing the stain color can go a very long way in buyer appeal.
3. Change the flooring: this can make a big difference but often at a big price.
4. Change the cabinet hardware: a simple and inexpensive update.
5. Change the backsplash: since backsplashes timestamp a kitchen, updating a backsplash can update a kitchen.
6. Change the lighting: change outdated fixtures.

Unless you're planning on staying in your home for a few more years before you sell—or you're a house flipper—it usually doesn't make sense to renovate the whole kitchen. Just choose a few updates. Talk to your home stager and real estate agent and choose the updates that give you the most impact for your buck.

In the example above, I was the home seller. When I bought this house, I planned on living in it for five or six years, so when I made updates to the house, I did them with staging in mind and chose styles that were just beginning to trend at the time and would likely last at least another five years. The cabinets were fairly new, but the cherrywood color was a style that was already out of date in my market. So I painted them white, which brightened up the kitchen a lot. Next, I added brass cabinet hardware and brass lighting, which was just coming into style at the time. The floor tile was changed, and a subway tile backsplash added. All of these updates were inexpensive compared to a complete renovation but had the same impact—and they made me happy when I was living there. Then, when I put the house on the market six years later, I received three offers over list price in the first week. It pays to think ahead to the resale appeal of any renovations that you make.

BEFORE

AFTER

This kitchen was in a large house, and it was small and outdated. The neighborhood was high-end, so the reality was that the new homeowners would want to rip it out shortly after buying it. You may think that it's not worth putting money into this sort of project, since buyers will just renovate it anyway. But most buyers can't see past outdated key rooms, especially in a house with a high price tag. *More importantly, with the kitchen left as is, a lot of potential buyers would just walk away from the house because they'd be turned off by the hassle of having to renovate a kitchen immediately after buying the house.* By doing some inexpensive renovations, keeping the budget in mind at all times, you can do a simple update that retains a lot of buyers who may otherwise be turned away, thereby making back any money you spend and then some, increasing your chance of getting more offers and, depending on the market, a bidding war. The buyers of this minimally updated kitchen may also think that they would like to renovate, but they would be content to live with the kitchen as it stands while they settle in, get their new life started, get plans drawn up, and talk to contractors.

In this example, the updates chosen were a new backsplash, painting existing kitchen cabinets, new counters, sink, and faucet, new hardware for the cabinets, and lighting.

Money-Saving Tip!

Replacing old kitchen and bathroom cabinet handles is an effective and inexpensive update.

Tiles Are a Timestamp

By looking at the tiles in a house, you can tell when the house was built or last renovated. Small glass tiles, large porcelain floor tiles, pastel-colored ceramic tiles, and graphic encaustic tiles have all been popular at various times and speak to the time when a home was built or last renovated. And like any fashion, if they've been out long enough, tile styles come back again, like subway tiles, for example.

So when it comes to updating a room, it often makes sense to change tiles. But changing tiles isn't as quick and easy as, say, taking down outdated drapery. It can be expensive, so it's not necessarily something you might do when staging a home, but, depending on the house and the market you're selling in, it can often be very worthwhile. Since the tile probably covers the whole floor or a full backsplash, you can completely change the room by making this change.

Big-box hardware stores often carry a combination of new, on-trend tiles and gone-out-of-style-ten-years-ago tiles. Be careful that you choose the newer on-trend tiles. Do five minutes of homework and search tile trends, or outdated tiles, so you can make an informed decision when you choose the new tiles.

BEFORE

AFTER

In the example on the previous page, the kitchen felt very outdated. The floor tiles were ugly (I'm sorry, but I don't know how else to describe them), and the backsplash tiles probably looked cute when they were installed, but to the target market buyer for this house, they were unappealing. By taking out the floor tiles (in this case, we decided to extend the hardwood floors from the adjoining family room) and replacing the backsplash, as well as painting the cabinets and replacing the counters, the kitchen was completely transformed. Changing these surface details made the kitchen very appealing to buyers and actually changed the feel of the whole house, since it was located in the center of the home. Because of these factors, and the fact that this was a key room, this minor renovation made a lot of sense to do. The sellers had multiple offers over their asking price and made back the money they had spent on the renovation—and a whole lot more.

When your budget or the price point of your home doesn't allow for replacing the tiles, there are still good alternatives to consider. Tile decals can be purchased and simply stuck over existing tiles or drywall, and they can look great. Adhesive contact paper can do the same thing. It comes in so many patterns and colors and is available at almost any hardware store. Not only can it be used on backsplashes and as frosting on windows, but it can be used inside drawers and cabinets as well.

Always remember, you're not doing updates with your style preferences in mind; you're doing what the new buyers like. When in doubt, get something light and neutral and very plain. Because tiles are difficult to change once they're laid, you're much, much wiser to choose a tile that's plain and boring—not taste specific. Then you're less likely to turn anyone off. You can add visual interest elsewhere, such as accessories that can be easily moved and changed. Keep the tiles light, plain—and if they seem boring, you've got the right ones.

Contact paper was used here to cover an outdated tile backsplash for an inexpensive update.

The Secret to Updates That Sell Your Home: Spend Wisely

Don't spend money on updates that won't be appreciated by buyers. Concentrating on curb appeal, foyers, and kitchen and bathroom updates is usually a safe bet, but consult with a home stager and your real estate agent—they should know your market and what buyers are looking for. Get pricing on the updates you're considering, and don't overspend for your home's price point. Make less expensive updates a priority and consult with your agent before committing to the more expensive ones.

Bathroom Updates on a Budget

Is your bathroom sad-looking and outdated? If you're flipping a house or in a high-end market, you may need to do a complete renovation. But, for most homeowners, that's not the case. Most buyers want to move in right away, so you will severely limit your pool of buyers if you leave bathrooms looking dated or in need of repairs.

So your goal with bathroom updates is to improve them enough that buyers will think, "It's not my dream bathroom, but at least we don't need to renovate before moving in. We can easily live with it and then renovate it after living in the home for a while." The last thing you want is for your potential buyers to think they would need to renovate before they move in.

Bathrooms are often easily transformed with simple updates. Here are some I recommend.

1. If your base cabinet is outdated or in need of major repair, consider replacing it with a new one from one of the big-box stores. You can find some that include a sink and counter for a really great price. They offer current styles and colors that are on trend, and those will make a good impression on buyers.

2. If your counter and sink are in good shape and not outdated, but the base needs an update, consider painting the base white and adding new hardware.

3. Tubs, sinks, and tiles that are brown (or other dated colors) can be glazed white. When in doubt about any colors in a bathroom, go white! White tiles, white floors, white tub—the whiter, the better. White says clean and fresh to buyers. And clean and fresh sells houses.

4. If your faucets and hardware are '80s brass, replace them. Yes, brass came back, but it's a different brass that's not as shiny. '80s brass really turns buyers off.

5. Do you have a medicine cabinet over the sink that is looking shabby? Don't replace it, since a more updated look usually doesn't include a medicine cabinet. Patch and paint the wall after you remove the cabinet, and place a mirror (perhaps a round one) over the sink.

If your bathroom has been updated in the past ten years and it's in good shape, then leave it alone. However, if it's been longer, you should consider doing some simple updates.

Updating Tip!

On average, home buyers are younger than home sellers. The age group that buys the most houses is from thirty to thirty-eight years of age so it often makes sense to update for a younger buyer's taste.

Source: 2020 Home Buyer and Sellers Generational Trends Report by the National Association of REALTORS® Research Group.

Here are two examples of bathrooms that have been refreshed and updated on a budget. The original bathrooms would have been turnoffs for prospective buyers, but it didn't make sense for the home sellers to completely gut these rooms. It would have cost them a lot of money and, in consultation with their real estate agent, we determined that it wasn't likely that they would get all of that money back in an increased sale price.

The result may not be the buyer's idea of a dream bathroom, but the transformation was enough so that buyers wouldn't feel like they would have to renovate before they moved in.

BATHROOM 1:

This bathroom had not been updated in about forty years. Everything about it was tired-looking, and it would have been a definite turnoff for buyers. So the goal was to refresh the room so that it was more inviting by replacing the features that needed it most.

The vanity was in disrepair and very low. Luckily, new vanities with sinks can be found at big-box stores for a great price. This one was on sale at the time, and a new faucet was added too. The medicine cabinet was outdated and in disrepair, so it was removed. Medicine cabinets were not on trend at the time anyway, so the wall was patched and painted and a wall-mount mirror added. New light fixtures, a new shower curtain and rod, and the update was complete.

The floor tile was garish, but it was in good shape, so it stayed. The beige wall tiles were also in good shape, so they stayed too; same for the toilet and tub. But you can see the difference that was made and imagine how it would make the home feel more move in ready!

BEFORE

AFTER

BATHROOM 2:

Does this bathroom need a makeover? Yes. In the high-end market where this home was listed, buyers would look at it and run. But it wasn't a key room, so it didn't make sense to spend a lot of money there. By painting the cabinets, adding a new Formica countertop, sink, and faucet, and updating the mirror and lighting, the bathroom feels updated and much more welcoming—with very little money spent.

Remember: it's often not necessary to do a complete renovation to update—the key is to do some easy updates so that buyers don't feel they need to renovate before they move in. If that happens, you've probably lost them!

Five Low-Cost Updates That Help Sell Homes

1. Painting over outdated colors.
2. Replacing light fixtures.
3. Removing outdated window treatments.
4. Minor kitchen remodels.
5. Minor bathroom remodels.

Window Treatments

Updating Tip!

Removing outdated window treatments goes a long way toward creating a fresh new look. Unless you need them for your own privacy or sun blocking, it's not necessary to replace them with new ones—just clean the windows so they'll let in a lot of gorgeous light.

Window treatments are like anything else in interior design. One year they're in; a few years later, they're out. Yet most people install new window treatments once—when they buy the house—and never update them. In the '90s and early 2000s, when the Tuscan look was popular, the trend in window coverings included heavy valances and heavy lined curtains (preferably silk). There are a lot of homes now that still have this look, but it is a dated look that isn't appealing to most buyers now—and it just doesn't work at all for staging. The people who have these heavy curtains often spent a lot of money on them, so they are understandably often reluctant to take the treatments down. If you are in this position, the good news is that this is one of the easiest and most affordable updates you can do. Just by taking the heavy curtains down, you change the feel of your room.

The bonus is that, by taking these curtains down, you'll let in *so* much light. It's surprising how much light gets blocked. So your room will feel a lot brighter and more appealing to buyers.

In regard to valances and draped window scarves, take them down even if the material is not heavy. They date the look of a room and do not increase the appeal of your home to today's buyers. Vertical blinds went out a long time ago, so take them down too.

If privacy isn't an issue, you don't need any window treatments at all. Just leave the windows bare and let the light in. If you need something for privacy, keep it light and be sure you are able to pull the treatment back to expose the whole window. Have a look on social media to see what is trending and aim for that look. And don't spend a lot of money on your window treatments—the detailing doesn't matter so much. It's the overall look that counts.

Before and after photos of family room. This gorgeous home badly needed an update and was languishing on the market without any interest. When called in to stage it, I removed the outdated drapery, chose an on-trend paint color, and brought in updated, more casual furniture that appealed to the target buyer. Result: immediate sale!

Lighting Updates

Lighting fixtures are often compared to jewelry. They are the one of the finishing touches that can be small but have a big impact. Consider updating your light fixtures, especially in your key rooms. Here are some lighting updates that are common when staging.

DINING ROOM PENDANTS:

These fixtures are often the focal point of the dining room, so it can be a good idea to update these.

TRACK LIGHTING:

If you've got 1970s original track lighting in poor condition, consider replacing it with some new LED track lighting. It will brighten the room and update it at the same time. Or remove the track lighting and replace it with something different, maybe a combination of a pendant and some task lighting. Just because track lighting made sense in the '70s, it doesn't mean you need to stick with it.

'80S LIGHTING:

If your standing lamp looks like it belongs in a *Miami Vice* episode, it probably isn't the best lighting for staging. Replace it with some updated fixtures to increase buyer appeal.

LAMP SHADES:

Like everything else, lamp shade shapes have trends too. So by simply switching out the lamp shades on your existing lamps, you can update your look. Also, dark-colored lamp shades can fade and white shades can yellow; by removing them and adding a fresh new lamp shade, the whole lamp can look brand-new.

OUTDOOR LIGHTING:

With outdoor lighting, you may not want the latest trend, but something that matches the style of your home. For instance, if your home is an Arts and Crafts style home, then it makes sense to have lighting that's that style too. By having well-maintained lighting that matches the style of your home, you can boost your curb appeal.

Eight Common Updates for Outdated Rooms

1. Take down heavy drapes and all valances.
2. Remove old wallpaper.
3. Paint walls in light neutrals.
4. Remove wall-to-wall carpeting.
5. Update lighting.
6. Paint kitchen cabinets.
7. Update outdated tiles.
8. Change cabinet hardware.

Wall Updates Are Big

Walls are one of the simplest things to update, and because they are physically so large, when you change them, it has a dramatic effect on the look of your home. Take down outdated wallpaper, wallpaper borders, and remove old faux finishes, stenciling, and old paint colors. Red walls were popular in the early 2000s, grays were popular in the 2010s. When your walls are out of date, your whole home looks dated.

Before and after photos of bedroom. The wallpaper in this room would have really distracted potential buyers. Using the same furniture, the room was transformed with fresh paint, and new bedding and accessories.

Interior Paint Colors

Choosing paint colors can be overwhelming, and it is easy to choose the wrong ones, even if you are just sticking with white. There are thousands of colors to choose from, and I recommend that you pay for a color consultation from your local stager or designer. A good color consultation will leave you with a staging-friendly paint color plan for all of the walls, ceilings, and trim, and for the exterior of your home as well.

However, if you are not able to arrange for a color consultation, here are some things to consider when choosing your staging paint colors:

1. Stick with light, neutral colors.
2. Research which neutrals are currently on trend by doing a quick online search.
3. In kitchens and bathrooms, choose wall colors that work with the undertones of the tiles, counters, floors, and cabinets. For instance, if your backsplash and counters are tiles and stone that have green undertones, you'll want to choose a light neutral that works with those green undertones.
4. Keep floor color in mind: if your beige tiles have pink undertones, you don't want to choose a neutral with yellow undertones. Choose a white or cream that has a *very* subtle matching undertone.

5. Keep things simple. The trim colors and the ceiling colors can be the same throughout the home.

6. Wall colors should flow from room to room and work with each other. When you hold the swatches of the paint colors for all of the rooms together, they should look nice together. No color should feel like it doesn't belong with the others. The exception for this would be children's bedrooms, but even there, it is better to keep them neutral and let the accessories be colorful.

7. Paint is not a selling feature, so in most cases, let it play a back seat. However, it *can* be used for dramatic effect to highlight a selling feature. If you have a gorgeous fireplace or woodwork detailing that you want to stand out so that buyers notice it, choose contrasting neutrals so that those selling features stand out, as in the photo below.

8. Before painting, prepare the wall by taking down all of the existing nails and hooks, and patching the holes left behind. You'll probably want to remove a lot of the photos and artwork when you style the room, so take them out before you paint. Also remove any phone jacks, wiring, and cables that are no longer live.

9. Choose the correct paint sheens. *Woodwork and trim:* semi-gloss. *Ceilings:* Flat or ceiling paint. *Walls in kitchens and baths:* Pearl. *Walls in other rooms of the home:* Eggshell—or Flat if the walls are in bad shape, you're painting with a dark color, or the room is in a low-traffic area.

Four Reasons to Get a Paint Color Consultation

1. To save you the stress of the decision-making.
2. To save you money in wasted paint if you choose the wrong color.
3. To save you time in repainting over bad color choices.
4. To achieve your goal of appealing to buyers and increasing the value of your home, which is the whole reason to do it in the first place.

Exterior Paint Colors

Exterior paint colors should also be neutral—unless you live in a part of the world where it is the norm to have brightly colored homes. When choosing your exterior paint colors, here are the guidelines to help you out.

1. Take stock of any fixed features such as stone, brickwork, the roof, and anything else that won't be painted. Your new paint colors will need to go well with these features.

2. Choose the main color. If the majority of your exterior is being painted, choose an on-trend neutral that works with your fixed features.

3. Choose an accent color. This is typically applied to the front door and/or shutters. This can be a neutral color that is either a lot darker or lighter than the main color of your home, or this can be where you add a pop of color.

4. Choose a trim color. This is usually a light neutral that works with your main color.

5. Consider the architectural style of your home. Different styles of home look better with different palettes. Look at similar homes in your neighborhood and online to see what looks best.

6. Most paint companies have "historic" lines of paint that are more subtle and complex than the rest of their line. Choosing one of these colors is often a safer bet and avoids garish colors that would look out of place in most communities.

7. Paint colors react differently to the light outside than they do to indoor light, so don't assume that a color that works in one of the rooms in your home will also work on the exterior of your home.

Flooring Updates

These home sellers made the decision to replace their carpeting with new wood floors and they were glad they did; their house had many offers and sold for over list price.

By updating your floors, you will increase the scope of buyers interested in your home. Floor updates are easily noticed in online photos and will draw more buyers to your home. Here are some updates that appeal to buyers.

Updating Tip!

Old sofas can be updated with new throw pillows for an easy new look.

1. Remove wall-to-wall carpet. If you have wood floors under your carpet, you will instantly update the look of your home by getting rid of the carpet and exposing your floors. If you don't have wood floors under the carpet, it can still pay to remove the carpet and lay down new carpet (see Budgeting for Updates, below).

2. Add tiles that are on trend. As I said, tiles timestamp a home's latest renovation. So if you add tiles that are currently trending, your house will feel very current and you will increase its appeal. If your budget for updates is low and your home is not in the luxury market, peel-and-stick tiles can be a great alternative.

3. Cover any dated flooring with an alternative modern flooring. See page 59 for more flooring information.

Here's a cautionary tale of what not to do. I once met with a family who were about to sell a house that was full of historic charm but hadn't been updated for many years, and everything was worn looking. Before I was called there to do a staging consultation, they had been proactive and had done some interior repairs and upgrading to get the house ready for sale. When I came to do the consultation, I realized they had just installed new wall-to-wall carpeting throughout the entire home (which buyers hate), covering up beautiful pine wide-plank floors (which buyers love). It was such a shame! They had spent a lot of money to cover up a wonderful selling feature—money they could have put toward other needed repairs and modernizing which would have resulted in a much higher ROI. The moral of the story: Have a staging consultation *before* you start repairs and updates, and the consultation fee will pay for itself many times over.

Budgeting for Updates

In all cases, money should only be spent on updates when it is determined that the amount that you spend on them will likely increase the price of your home by more than the amount that you spend.

For example, if your kitchen badly needs an update and your real estate agent or home stager advises that it is likely that an updated kitchen would increase the sellability of your home and your list price by $40,000, spending $10,000 to $20,000 on well-planned updates is a smart decision.

Every market and every house is different. So in some instances, it makes sense to do more expensive updates and, in other instances, the bare minimum should be spent.

Summary

- Choose updates that will appeal to your target buyer.
- Updating your key rooms will help your home sell for more.
- It can sometimes make sense to spend money on updating rooms that the buyer will renovate after they move in.
- Updating paint colors has a large impact.
- Spending money wisely on updates will result in a great return on your investment.

Step Three:
Depersonalize

Depersonalizing is an important task and is one of the big differences between home staging and interior design or decorating. Whereas interior design is personal and taste specific, home staging design is the opposite as much as possible. There isn't a home going on the market that can't benefit from at least a little depersonalization. It's an extremely effective home staging step, and the good news is that it can be done by any homeowner. And it's a marketing tool recommended by every home stager and any savvy real estate agent.

So What Exactly Is Depersonalizing?

Depersonalizing is the process of removing the elements from a home that make it personally appealing to the home seller, with the goal of creating a broad appeal to the greatest possible number of home buyers. By presenting more of a blank slate to buyers, it allows them to easily imagine living in the home with their own personal style and reduces any emotional turnoffs buyers might experience.

Keep in mind that the majority of potential buyers looking at your home will probably have completely different taste than you do, and they may even be from a different generation. If your home is very taste specific, you'll turn off a lot of buyers. You may think that these buyers should be smart enough to look past your things and just see the actual home. But in reality, buyers are very, very affected by the belongings and style of the home seller. 90 percent of people cannot look past what they see and will not be able to imagine your home looking any different from how you show it to them. So do yourself a favor and make it as little taste specific as possible so that you appeal to the greatest number of people. You'll be much more likely to receive multiple offers and sell quickly.

When choosing a home to buy, buyers are not basing their decision solely on practical considerations—it is also a very emotional decision. They want to fall in love with a home, so make it easy for them to fall in love with *your* home! Increase the value of your home by widening its appeal and removing as many of the personal details as possible.

The Secret to Depersonalizing: Speed

Since depersonalizing requires identifying personal items, your emotions are bound to be triggered by them, and it's easy to get sidetracked. But spending hours sorting through old photos and memorabilia is not a good use of your time when getting your home ready for sale. It's important that you spend your house prep time wisely, depersonalize quickly, and move on to other ways to increase the perceived value and appeal of your home. After all, depersonalizing doesn't mean throwing out your personal items—you're just prepacking them. Get it done quickly and move on to something else, such as replacing the leaky faucet in your kitchen or painting the walls a staging-friendly color.

Personal Photos

Money-Saving Tip!

Depersonalizing your home is the cheapest and easiest way to increase the appeal and perceived value of your home.

Taking down personal photos is one of the fastest and most effective ways to depersonalize your home. All you need to do is gather them up and prepack them. You'll need to pack your photos up at some point anyway, so do it before you go on the market and you'll take a big step toward depersonalizing your home. Go from room to room and gather up all of your family photos from the walls and tops of furniture. Then wrap them carefully and put them all in labeled cartons.

I highly recommend doing this quickly and without a lot of thought. You can decide what to keep and what to display in your new home when you get there. The reason I say this is that photos can bring up a lot of emotional responses and if you start to think about them, it can take *forever* to do this simple task. So for now, just focus on getting them all packed. Set a timer for five or ten minutes, go through the house quickly, and gather them up and put them in a big pile. Then just wrap them and box them up. Label the boxes, put the boxes away, and cross that off your list.

If you're planning on downsizing and won't have room to display as many of your personal photos in your new home, make two piles. The first pile can be for photos that you definitely won't display after you move. Take these photos out of the frames, put all the photos in one box or large envelope, and label it. Then put the empty frames in your give-away pile (or, if they are damaged, recycle them or throw them out). The second pile can be for photos that you might display in your new home. Again, don't think about this too much. If you're not sure if you'll want to display it, just put it in the second pile anyway. You'll be able to make these more emotional decisions when you're living in your new space and have all of your furniture set up.

We all move for different reasons, and if your upcoming move will likely be a very emotional and trying experience, it might be important to keep some meaningful items at hand. If you have one or two photos that you don't want to live without while you're selling and you don't want to prepack them, of course that's okay. Consider keeping them out on display so you can see them most of the time, and then tucking them out of sight in a drawer when potential buyers come. Some real estate agents tell all their clients that it's okay to keep some photos out, but I say, why would you? Allowing potential buyers every opportunity to imagine themselves living in the space translates into more sales. You can put them back out again when the buyers are gone.

Depersonalizing Tip!

Here is an alternative to removing a framed personal photo from your wall. Take the frame off the wall, slide something into the frame in front of the photo—maybe a page from an art book, an old map, pretty wrapping paper, or a calendar photo—and hang the frame back up.

But here is one possible exception to the no-personal-photos rule: if you can use an aspirational photo to actually help buyers imagine themselves living the life *they* dream of. In this case, the photo is a prop rather than something personal of yours. Remember, you are not just selling a home, you are selling a lifestyle. For example, if you live by the ocean and you have a nice, small photo of the nearby beach or a sailboat, that could help buyers imagine that sort of lifestyle. But be sure that the boat, beach, or ocean are the prominent subject of the photo and that it isn't really just a photo of you and your friends and family smiling for the camera. Think of what might be drawing potential buyers to your area and help remind them of that feature when they are in your home. It's best if it's a recreational feature. It might be a selling feature for a city home to be near a subway stop, but that doesn't really make for a good photo. A picture of the park nearby would be better.

If you have a lot of photos on your walls, you will be left with a lot of holes in the walls when you take them down. You may be left with a lot of patching, sanding, and painting to be done—which is not a problem if the walls need painting anyway. But if the paint and the walls are otherwise in good shape, and the paint color is already staging-friendly (see page 87), you don't want to have to patch and paint the whole wall unnecessarily. Here are two suggestions to avoid repainting the whole wall.

1. If the holes are small, you can fill them with a dab of matching paint. Use a cotton swab or a fine artist brush and put a tiny bit of paint in the hole without putting any paint on the wall itself. If some paint does get on the wall, wipe it off. Wait for it to dry and see if you might need to do it a second time. It's important that the paint is the same color and sheen as the paint on the walls. If you kept the leftover paint when you painted the walls, it won't be a problem.

2. If the holes are too big to try the first tip, here is a trick that one of my clients told me about: first fill the small holes with toothpaste (I'm not kidding). The paste style, not gel. Again, fill in the hole only with the toothpaste; wipe off any that gets on the wall. Then, when the toothpaste is dry and level with the wall, carefully dot some matching paint on top of the toothpaste with a cotton swab or very small paint brush. My client did a great job using this method! If you knew exactly where to look, you could see it, but if you didn't know that the toothpaste-paint combo was there, you would never notice it.

The shelves in this home were depersonalized before going on the market. The home seller also anticipated buying new furniture for her next home, so she bought it early and used it for staging her home.

Do your walls and furniture look empty now that you've removed your personal photos? Good! Remember, with staging, less is more. You want less on the walls that you would normally have when you are living in a home. If you have some completely empty walls, that's okay. Just a few pieces of artwork, strategically placed, is ideal. You can read more about what to have on your walls, and how much, on page 163.

Collections

Personal collections of any sort should be packed up and put away. Why? The obvious reason is because they are personal and your goal in staging is to depersonalize, of course!

Just a few examples of personal collections I've come across while staging are: figurine collections, model train collections, coin collections, mug collections, shot glass collections, snow globes, sports memorabilia, hats, baseball caps, animals, magazines, rock band memorabilia, souvenirs and artwork from travels, empty wine bottles (presumably from special occasions), and so many corks! Why are people reluctant to throw out corks?

Let's say that you love frogs and have frog figurines, frog towels, frog oven mitts, and frog photos on the walls. When your birthday comes around, your friends know to get you something with a frog on it. That's great! You love them, and maybe your family loves them, so of course you will take them with you when you move. But most people don't collect frogs and will not love them like you do. Home sellers have said to me that, if buyers don't like their house with all the personal details present, then they don't want to sell to them. That's their prerogative, but it really limits their pool of interested buyers. Do you only want to sell your house to people who feel that passionately about frogs? Or your favorite football team? If you leave these things on display while you're selling, you will turn off a lot of buyers who can't make a personal connection to your house because they have a hard time seeing past your collections.

Prepack all of your collections so that buyers don't get distracted by them. You want them to notice your home, not your stuff.

If you've picked up souvenirs from your travels that are particular to the places you've visited, those things are personal and should generally be packed up.

One house I staged had giraffes everywhere—probably about a hundred of them!—everything from small wooden giraffes on shelves to enormous giraffe sculptures in the backyard. There were giraffes hidden in closets, giraffe artwork on the walls, and giraffes standing in the living room. It was actually kind of cool, but if they had been left in the home while staging, buyers would have noticed all the giraffes when they should have been noticing the wood-burning fireplace and the great beams on the ceiling. So the giraffes were packed up, and the house sold right away.

Sports memorabilia should be packed up. What if a potential buyer hates your team? That buyer will have a bad taste in their mouth when they're in that room. Music tastes are personal too, so if you have rooms filled with music posters and memorabilia specific to certain bands or genres, pack that up as well. Political affiliations? Definitely prepack any political items and aim to appeal to buyers in all political parties.

If you're an avid crafter and have examples of your craft prominently displayed—whether it's quilts, pottery, stained glass, or anything else—it's still personal and you'd be wise to pack them up and get them ready for their new home. A craft area can be a selling feature, but the crafts themselves are often a personal labor of love that don't necessarily appeal to all buyers—especially if your target buyer is significantly younger or older than you are.

Will your home feel empty after you've done this? Yes, and that's okay. It's how you know you've done a good job.

Pro Tip!

"Your stager's number-one job is to recommend and implement changes to your house to make it emotionally connect to the widest audience of buyers possible. The flip side is you need to emotionally disconnect. Your memories will remain with you, but allowing buyers to see themselves in your house is why staging exists."

Peggy O'Connell
Inspired Home Staging
and Design
Northern Virginia
inspiredhomestaginganddesign.com

Trophies, Medals, Awards, and Plaques

Buyers respond better to homes that have the personal touches of the homeowner removed.

Like all personal things, trophies should be packed up. They are significant to the homeowner, but to the buyer, they just feel like clutter. That said, a small number *can* help when it comes to styling your home for staging if they help remind buyers of selling features of your neighborhood. For example, if you have golf courses nearby and you have some golf trophies, placing one or two of them in an office will help remind buyers of the nearby golf courses. Buyers might aspire to a life in which they play more golf, so this helps them visualize this. In this way, you are using the trophy as a prop, which is different from displaying the trophies as your own accomplishments.

Kids often get an enormous number of trophies. When the trophies are crowding shelving or dresser tops, from a staging perspective, they are cluttering the room. Prepack the ones your child wants to keep in the new home and discard the rest. Of course, if your child has a hard time with this, don't traumatize them. Just remove as many as they are comfortable with.

Awards, medals, and commemorative plaques should all be pre-packed. Unless you've been awarded something that somehow helps sell the house itself or the surrounding area, prepack these items for your next home.

Money-Saving Tip!

Depersonalizing your home is the easiest and cheapest way to increase the appeal and value of your home.

Religious Items

Religions are a very important part of many people's lives, but they are deeply personal and don't have a role in staging. Wars have been fought over them. Unless you live in an area where 100 percent of your prospective buyers practice the same religion you do, prepack any references to your own religion and spiritual beliefs. If you'd like to keep some smaller items for prayer or reference while your home is on the market, put them out of sight in a drawer or other convenient place where they won't be seen by prospective buyers.

Interior and Exterior Paint Colors

Money-Saving Tip!

Overwhelmed with the amount of painting you need to do? Concentrate on the key rooms.

One of the most important aspects of depersonalizing your home is the removal of strong taste-specific paint colors, especially in key rooms. Colors are personal—everyone likes and dislikes different colors. You may love your red walls, but it's a safe bet that there will be prospective buyers that don't.

Do you need to depersonalize the paint color of the exterior of your home? Paint color on the exterior is just as important as (or even more important than) the colors of your house's interior. Is your house a distinctive color that is a little unusual for your area? Is it a dated color? Do people often comment on it? Time to paint! For help on the choosing the right color combination, refer to page 89.

It's great to personalize your home with your favorite colors when you live in it, like in this purple kitchen. But before you put your home on the market, change those personal favorite touches to colors that appeal to the widest number of buyers.

If painting for future owners sounds like a lot of bother, here are four reasons why it's worth your time and money to replace your strong paint colors with staging-friendly neutrals:

1. YOU'LL ELIMINATE THE RISK OF TURNING BUYERS OFF.

Can't buyers just see past the color of your walls? No. They can't and they won't. Color invokes unconscious emotions, some of which are negative. You want buyers to fall in love with your home, not strain to see past paint colors that they don't like.

2. YOU'LL UPDATE YOUR HOME.

Color trends come and go. If your paint colors are out of style, your entire home will feel dated and its value will be reduced. (See Step Two.)

3. YOU'LL GET BUYERS TO NOTICE WHAT'S IMPORTANT.

Strong colors distract from your home's selling features. Do you want buyers turning their nose up at the wall colors or paying attention to your important selling features? If you've ever watched a TV show about buying homes, you've seen buyers focusing on paint colors they don't like, to the detriment of the home's sale.

4. YOU'LL INCREASE THE MOVE-IN READINESS OF YOUR HOME.

By painting on-trend light neutrals throughout your home, you've just created another selling feature for your home. Any potential buyer will love that they don't have a painting project to tackle in their immediate future.

Use this effective marketing technique to more effectively sell your home. For help in choosing the right colors, see page 87.

Money-Saving Tip!

Increase your home's equity by decreasing your personal touches.

Curb Appeal

There are so many ways that homeowners personalize their properties and the exterior of their homes. I've been focusing on the interior up until now, but of course the exterior is the first thing buyers will see. So don't forget to depersonalize outside too! Remove any lawn ornaments, personal details, or whimsical features on your home's exterior and the property itself.

Here are ten things to prepack when depersonalizing your exterior:

1. Front door decoration
2. Flags and banners, whether political or decorative
3. Wind catchers, wind chimes, wind spinners, pinwheels
4. Mirror balls
5. Decorative plaques with inspirational sayings

6. Statues of lions, eagles, rabbits, toads, cranes, or any other animals—large or small

7. Angels, saints, mezuzahs, buddhas, or other religious items

8. Decorative mailbox covers

9. Gnomes, trolls, leprechauns, fairies, faux toadstools

10. Decorative wishing wells

Summary

- Depersonalizing is an inexpensive, effective marketing tool that helps sell your home.

- Prepack all personal photos, collections, crafts, souvenirs, trophies, and political and religious items.

- Replace strong paint colors with staging-friendly neutrals.

- Don't forget to depersonalize the exterior of your home as well as the interior!

Step Four: Declutter— Reduce and Simplify

About the Words "Clutter" and "Decluttering"

To most people, the word "clutter" has negative implications. For a home stager to say that a home seller's belongings are "clutter" can sound judgmental and obnoxious. Therefore, "reduce and simplify" is a term widely used by home stagers because it is less negative than "decluttering" and more instructional—and it specifies exactly what tasks need to be done. However, I personally do use the terms clutter and declutter simply because, when it comes to selling a home, the role of a home stager is to look at the home from the buyer's perspective in order to help the sale. And the truth is, to the buyer, the current homeowners' things *do* feel like clutter and often get in the way of a fast, high sale. Also, homes that are filled with a lot of belongings do look cluttered in online photography. So please know that, when I use these terms, I use them with the intention of helping a home sell, not as a judgment on how people actually live. Everyone needs to reduce and simplify before selling their home.

So, if all homes that are occupied (lived in) while on the market need to be decluttered, but a completely empty home doesn't sell as well either, you might wonder, how many pieces of furniture and accessories are needed to be optimal for a sale? The answer is, you need to keep enough furniture to show the use of each space effectively and enough accessories to do so in an attractive manner—no more. Even the homes of people who live fairly minimalist and "clutter-free" can usually benefit from some further minimizing and prepacking.

Why Declutter?

Home staging is a powerful marketing tool, and decluttering is a key component of this tool. What makes it so important? Why do buyers like it so much?

Decluttering helps sell your home in four important ways:

1. It dramatically improves the look of your marketing photos.
2. It makes each room feel larger, cleaner, and more inviting to a potential buyer.
3. It allows buyers to appreciate the house itself without getting distracted by a home seller's belongings.

The Secret to Decluttering: Prepack

Decluttering for staging is different from normal decluttering in one big way: when you declutter for staging, you don't need to get rid of anything. You just need to prepack some of your things for your move. The goal at this time is to make your home appealing to buyers—not to organize for how you live. You can do that when you get to your new place and see what works and fits in your new space.

4. It provides more of a blank canvas for potential buyers to imagine themselves living in the home.

While the purpose of the decluttering is to get top dollar for your home, you may also find that it has some positive side effects for you personally. After working with many clients who have decluttered their homes with staging in mind, most of those people discovered that they *loved* having their home less cluttered and decided to adopt this new way of living in their next home. Many homeowners find that, by decluttering and living with only those things that they use often and that bring them joy (thank you, Marie Kondo!), they experience some or all of the following benefits:

1. They feel more relaxed, calmer, and even happier while in their home.

2. They spend less time searching for things.

3. They spend less money because they can actually find the things they already own and therefore don't need to buy as much.

4. They have less to clean and maintain.

And even those home sellers who don't love the more minimalist style of living achieved by decluttering definitely appreciate that they have already done a lot of their packing and have increased the appeal of their home.

How to Declutter for Staging

There are many methods for decluttering your home, so if you have the time to read some books or watch YouTube videos on this subject, it can be helpful. But one very important thing to keep in mind is that most decluttering techniques apply to people reducing and organizing items in their lives in general. Selling your home can be a very busy time, and you will probably have a lot of other important things to do besides decluttering. So it's not usually the best use of your time to determine whether each item that you own should come or go, whether it sparks joy, or how best to organize things.

Did You Know?

95 percent of agents recommend that home sellers declutter their home before putting it on the market.

Source: 2019 Profile of Home Staging, National Association of REALTORS® Research Group.

To get the best price for your home, spend as much of your free time as possible on repairs, updates, and styling that will increase the equity and appeal of the fixed assets of your home. This is *not* the best time for sorting and organizing. Do your decluttering and depersonalizing quickly, without a lot of thought and with as little emotional engagement as possible, so that you get the maximum return for your time spent.

Decisions about what to keep are best made when you're unpacking in your new home. The quicker you can do your prepacking the better, so that you can cross it off your list and turn to other important staging tasks!

Decluttering Shelving

It is especially important to declutter your open shelves. A lot of people are shocked at how bad their full shelving can look in online photos. Even shelves that are kept neat and organized can look messy in a photo. Treat your open shelving as display areas rather than storage spaces.

Remove *at least* half of what you currently have on your shelves. It's even better if you remove almost everything and leave only a few decorative items. Do not be concerned if some of your open shelving is empty. Most books, especially tattered paperbacks and books with faded spines, should be removed. Also remove papers, magazines, workbooks and notebooks, knickknacks, collections, personal photos, and personal mementos. For information about how to style your shelves and make them look great for your staging, refer to page 184.

How to Schedule Your Decluttering and Other Staging Tasks

Decluttering Tip!

Start decluttering in the rooms that buyers will see first and then move on to the rest of the house. You'll feel good that you got the most important rooms done.

When it comes to decluttering for staging purposes, here is a fast, effective method that won't overwhelm you and will keep you organized and calm throughout the process:

STEP ONE: MAKE A SCHEDULE

Decide how many weeks or months it will be before you put your home on the market and divide your home into that number of zones. For instance, if you want to put your home on the market in five months, divide your home into five zones and tackle one zone per month.

In this example of five zones in five months, in an average-sized home, might look like this:

> Zone 1: Entry, living room, dining room
>
> Zone 2: Curb appeal, porch, front yard, back yard
>
> Zone 3: Kitchen
>
> Zone 4: Bathrooms
>
> Zone 5: Bedrooms

Each month, tackle one zone. You can allot time for decluttering as well as for any other work you'll need to do in that zone. Tackle the key rooms first and then move on to the less important zones after that.

STEP TWO: SET UP

You'll need the following supplies:

1. Cardboard boxes: get some free ones at a grocery or liquor store, or buy some from a moving supply store

2. Packing material for breakables

3. Packing tape to close the boxes

4. A thick marker to label boxes

5. Garbage bags for trash

6. Pen and paper or app for making lists

When you have your supplies, set up three receptacles in your Zone 1.

1. A box for prepacking items you will take to your new home

2. A box or large bag for donations

3. A large trash bag for garbage

STEP THREE: SET A TIMER FOR YOURSELF EVERY DAY

Each day, set a timer for a small, predetermined amount of time, and concentrate on decluttering as much as possible in that short space of time. I suggest ten or maybe fifteen minutes. Don't get distracted during that time—you can stay focused for ten minutes! You'll be surprised at how much you can get done. Just work as quickly as possible and stop when the timer is done.

Touch each item just once. Pick something up and put it directly into the appropriate box or bag. Don't make piles. For instance, if you are decluttering a closet, don't pull all the contents out onto the floor or bed. Just take out one item, determine its fate, and put it straight into the appropriate receptacle. When you have doubt about an item, simply put it in the prepacking box. It's better to do the majority of your sorting and organizing when you unpack in your new home. Then you'll know better how much space you have and where you want to put things. Remember: it's better to use any available time now on repairs, updating, painting, and styling.

When the timer goes off, label the outside of the box with the name of the room the items belong in using large letters, preferably with a thick marker. You can also list the contents as well. Alternatively, you can simply number each box and list the contents of each box digitally or on a piece of paper. That way, in the end, you have a master list of what is in each box which can help with the unpacking when you get to your new place.

If you have piles of things in corners that you have been meaning to get around to putting somewhere for some time, tackle those piles first, before closets and other closed spaces. Get your boxes, set your timer, and pack!

Do ten or fifteen minutes every day. You can do ten minutes a day. After one week of this method, you will be surprised at how much you have accomplished.

STEP FOUR: REMOVE YOUR BOXES AND BAGS AT LEAST ONCE A WEEK

At least once a week, store your pre-packed items in an out-of-the-way place. Most people rent a storage unit or a storage container. Do you have a friend or family member who has space in a garage or shed? If so, that can be helpful, and you can save some money on storage fees. Garages or storage areas in your home can be used too, if you can neatly stack the cartons, but avoid filling up any space that may be seen as a selling feature to a buyer. It's better to store boxes off-site if possible.

Removing your pre-packed boxes often will help you see your progress and allow you to continue to enjoy living in your home during the process.

How to Adapt This System for You

Every home is different and every person living in that home is different. So how might this method work for you? Here are three different situations to show how this method can be applied to different homes, different homeowners, and different time frames.

EXAMPLE ONE

Tamara has been in her home for eighteen years and raised her children there since they were babies. The home is fairly large, and she has accumulated a lot over that time, especially things the kids no longer need. She has a jam-packed basement, a full attic, and bursting closets, and her kitchen cabinets are full as well. She plans to put her home on the market in six months, so she divides her home into six zones, one for each month. The key rooms are prioritized as the first zones:

Zone 1: Front hall, living room, dining room

Zone 2: Kitchen and bathrooms

Zone 3: Primary suite and guest room

Zone 4: Family room, office

Zone 5: Kids' rooms

Zone 6: Basement rec room, laundry room, and storage

She decides that the attic will have to wait, since it's not as important to buyers' lifestyles, so she will tackle that later, while the home is on the market or after it is sold.

She has a full-time job and a limited amount of free time, so she decides to hire someone to do some painting and repairs and the gardening needed for curb appeal. She has a lot of prepacking to do and plans to donate a lot of things she and the kids no longer need. She allocates ten minutes at the end of each weekday, and one hour per day on weekends to do this. She sets a timer for the allotted time for that day and works quickly during that time. Any item that she is not sure whether to donate or not goes into a prepacking box to be sorted after her move.

Each Sunday, she loads the car with that week's cartons of donations and pre-packed items. She drives the pre-packed items to a nearby storage unit and the donations to a nearby charity. The garbage goes out on garbage day, and surprisingly quickly, her home becomes clutter-free and lighter. She doesn't feel stressed about the home preparation, since she has a plan and knows that she will have time to get to each room. She takes on a small amount each day, so she never feels overwhelmed. And she doesn't feel like her home has been overtaken by clutter since she doesn't have piles of things on the floor, couches, or beds, and she removes the things she's packed each week.

Early on, Tamara hired a local home stager, recommended by her real estate agent, for a staging consultation, so she has a plan for what furniture pieces she will be putting in storage, and she hires a mover to take those items to her storage unit. The stager has also chosen some fresh paint colors for key rooms and has indicated some of Tamara's accessories that might be useful in staging, so she knows not to prepack those items.

She finds that most of the zones are decluttered before the end of the month and spends the rest of the allocated time deep cleaning and organizing the repairs and painting done by local tradespeople. She also hires the stager to come back a few days before her home is to be photographed. The stager rearranges some furniture to improve the flow, adds fresh artwork and accessories, puts additional lighting in dark rooms, and styles each room to look its best.

After six months of sticking with a simple plan that wasn't stressful, Tamara's home looks great and will go for top dollar.

EXAMPLE TWO

Louis has lived in his one-bedroom apartment condominium for a little over three years. He lives on his own and is surprised at how much he has accumulated in that time. He plans to tackle the decluttering, painting, repairs, and cleaning himself. His real estate agent offers staging as part of her services, and she plans to add fresh artwork and accessories when Louis has done his "homework." He wants to put his condo on the market in one month, and his agent says that she will need the final week to do the staging and have the photography shot and the marketing materials and listing created. So Louis divides his home into three zones, one for each week available before the agent works her magic.

> Zone 1: Living room and entry
>
> Zone 2: Kitchen
>
> Zone 3: Bedroom and bathroom

Decluttering Tip!

Keep your packing, donating, and garbage receptacles in the zone you're currently working in. That way, your supplies are ready for you and it's easy to get started.

He decides to spend each week the following way:

Days 1, 2, 3: Fifteen minutes decluttering

Days 4, 5: Minor repairs and painting

Day 6: Deep cleaning

Day 7: Relax

After three weeks of working on his home in his spare time, he is ready for the agent to stage. She reviews the current listings of comparable condominiums in the area and is happy to see that Louis's listing will be far more appealing than the comps.

Seven Things You Can Do to Increase the Value of Your Home for No Money

1. Remove personal photos, collections, and memorabilia.
2. Declutter, inside and out.
3. Do a thorough deep clean, inside and out.
4. Remove odors (pets, mildew, cigarette smoke, food, etc.).
5. Maintain your home's exterior by mowing, watering, weeding, and tidying.
6. Before a showing, set your thermostat at a comfortable temperature.
7. Remove outdated valances and drapes.

EXAMPLE THREE

Gisele, Marion, Thomas, and two small children are an extended family that have lived in their three-bedroom home for eleven years. They plan on putting their home on the market in three months and divide their home into six zones, one for each two-week period. The three adults will do the work themselves in their spare time, and they assign each other specific tasks. Gisele will declutter and garden, Marion will paint, and Thomas will do repairs. They don't want to get in each other's way, so they each start in a different zone. Marion starts painting in Zone 1, since it needs the most painting, Thomas starts in Zone 2, since it needs the most repairs, and Gisele starts decluttering and gardening in Zone 3. They rotate zones each two-week period until the first three zones are done and move to the next three zones. Once they are finished with all six zones, they decide to add another two-week period to deep clean and style the home.

> Zone 1: Entry, living room, dining room
>
> Zone 2: Kitchen
>
> Zone 3: Exterior
>
> Zone 4: Bathrooms and main bedroom
>
> Zone 5: Remaining bedrooms

Within three and a half months, they are ready to put their house on the market, and their sweat equity translates into a top-dollar sale for their home.

Decluttering Checklist

FOYER/ENTRANCE

- Hall closet: remove enough coats so that the railing is about half full. Prepack out-of-season coats, accessories, and footwear. Reduce items on shelving and tidy up. Aim to make the floor bare and clean.
- Remove shoe racks, boot trays, footwear, umbrella holders, free-standing coat racks, key racks, and mail holders.
- Hooks by the door should be almost empty.
- Reduce and simplify furniture.
- Remove or replace mat on floor.

LIVING ROOM

- Reduce and simplify open shelving.
- Reduce and simplify furniture (see page 162 for advice on furniture arrangements).
- Remove all personal collections and photos.
- Remove rug if it is dated, dark, or stained.
- Remove heavy drapery and valances.

DINING ROOM

- Reduce and simplify furniture: Remove extra chairs; remove tall china cabinets; if a china cabinet is in two pieces and the top can be removed, keep the bottom part if the room is large enough and put the top in storage.

- Remove all personal collections and photos.

- Reduce and simplify any open shelving.

- Remove rug if it is dated, dark, or stained.

- Remove heavy drapery and valances.

KITCHEN

- Counters: remove almost all of the items on your counter, including dish rack, cutting boards, soaps, dish cloths, spoon rests, utensils, etc. Make space in the cabinets for these items.

- Reduce and tidy inside kitchen cabinets and drawers: buyers will look inside these spaces and they should appear roomy, not crowded.

Decluttering Tip!

Start your kitchen decluttering by prepacking any small appliances, large serving dishes, and "good" dishes you rarely use.

- Prepack anything you don't use on a regular basis.

- Glass-doored cabinets: reduce items here and arrange neatly.

- Tops of cabinets: remove all decorative or storage items.

- Fridge door: remove all magnets and personal items.

- Kitchen tables: clear, leaving one simple decorative item.

- Garbage can: put in a cabinet.

- Cork boards: reduce and simplify.

- Kitchen furniture: If there are any furniture pieces that you've added, like storage pieces, standalone shelving units, microwave stands, children's furniture, serving stands, extra stools, or chairs, remove these and put into storage.

FAMILY ROOMS, REC ROOMS, MEDIA ROOMS, AND OTHER RECREATIONAL INDOOR SPACES

Pro Tip!

"Selling a home where memories were made is very emotional. When I go to a staging consult, I like to see how long the homeowner has lived in their home. The longer they have lived there, the harder it is to say goodbye. Don't let 'holding on' cause you to lose a sale."

Julie Wills
Fresh Look, LLC
Spring Hill, TN

- Reduce and simply furniture, keep to a bare minimum, and put extra pieces in storage. If the space is large, such as a large finished basement, divide the space into smaller sections, such as one section for watching TV, another section with a ping pong or pool table, and another section with exercise equipment.

- Remove all storage items and bins.

- Depersonalize photos and collections.

- Clear tops of furniture.

- Declutter open shelving.

- Prepack videos, DVDs and CDs.

- Tidy gaming equipment and designate a basket or drawer to stow when showing home.

- Tidy wiring.

BEDROOMS

- Reduce and simplify furniture, keep to a bare minimum, and put extra pieces in storage.

- Remove any exercise equipment or office setup.

- Clear the tops of all furniture.

- Declutter open shelving.

- Reduce items in closet, clear the floor, tidy shelving.

- Remove personal items and photos.

- Remove or hide prescription drugs, jewelry, religious items, weapons, and valuables.

- Toys and gaming areas in children's bedrooms should be reduced and tidied. Put into storage whatever will not be played with in the next few months.

Decluttering Tip!

Start your closet decluttering by prepacking your out-of-season clothes, shoes, and outerwear.

OFFICE

- Clear desk.

- Box up any papers or files that you will not need in the near future.

- Reduce and simplify furniture.

- Remove plastic chair mats.

- Declutter shelving.

- Hide cords, wires, modems, etc.

- Replace oversized furniture with smaller-scale pieces.

- Remove calendars, diplomas, photos, and other personal items.

BATHROOMS

- Clear counter and sink completely. Put toothbrushes, toothpaste, soap, shaving items, makeup, and anything else you use regularly in a drawer or basket under the sink or in a nearby cabinet or closet.

- Remove bath mats and toilet seat covers.

- Hide plungers, toilet brushes, and garbage cans.

- Remove everything practical from open shelving; put only decorative plants or baskets here.

- Remove shower caddies.
- Reduce the products in a shower or bathtub to two or three (maximum) and hide these during photos.
- Remove all reading material and magazine racks.

Seven Things You Can Do to Increase the Value of Your Home—By Spending Five Hundred Dollars or Less

1. Paint key rooms.
2. Mulch beds and add flowers in key areas.
3. Replace old light bulbs.
4. Replace caulking in bathrooms.
5. Do needed minor repairs.
6. Update with fresh on-trend accessories.
7. Buy fresh white bedding and towels.

LAUNDRY AREA

- Completely clear open shelving, counters, tops of washer and dryer, and sink area.

- Remove any storage items, boxes, bins, cleaning products and tools, pet items or pet food, and clear the floor.

ATTICS, GARAGES, STORAGE ROOMS

- People want to see the space, not your stuff—so stack your storage items neatly along the sides. If it feels crowded, move some to a storage unit.

OUTSIDE

- Roll up hoses and store garden tools.
- Put garbage cans away.
- Put toys away.
- Remove empty flowerpots and containers.
- Remove worn or broken furniture.
- Remove taste-specific personal decorations (see page 106).
- Remove any dead or dying plants, bushes, trees.

Summary

- Decluttering helps sell your home in four important ways.
- Prepacking is the key to decluttering.
- Decluttering should be done quickly and without a lot of time spent on emotional triggers, so that you can spend more time on other staging tasks.
- Create a schedule for your decluttering and other staging tasks to reduce stress and achieve your goals.

Step Five:
Deep Clean

Clean Homes Attract Buyers and Sell Faster

What's different about cleaning your home for selling? It's cleaner! For maximum appeal, your home must be the cleanest it's ever been. Plan for a deep clean, targeting places you don't normally clean or even notice. Because, even if it feels clean to us, buyers will often notice dirt that we are blind to in our own homes—and other people's dirt is off-putting. They will not want to imagine themselves living in a home if it's dirty. Buyers love clean spaces and are instinctively drawn to immaculate homes, so putting in the effort for the extra cleaning is definitely worth it.

Increase the Equity of Your Home Without Spending Any Money

If you don't mind getting a little dirty, a deep clean is something that will cost you virtually nothing to do but will earn you a ton of equity! When you clean your home like it's never been cleaned before, every buyer that comes in the door is more likely to fall in love with your home. And by spending less than twenty dollars on cleaning products you can increase the value of your home by thousands of dollars. That's an amazing return on your investment!

Hiring a Cleaning Professional

Getting your home to the level of clean needed for a top sale can be difficult to achieve. So if you aren't able to do the deep cleaning yourself, it's worth the money to hire a professional cleaner. But be clear with your cleaner that you aren't looking for a regular maintenance clean; you'd like a deep clean. Make a list for them, using the checklist at the end of this chapter, so that your expectations are clear. Once the deep clean is done, you may also want to schedule regular maintenance cleanings to keep things ship-shape while you're on the market.

The Secret to Deep Cleaning: Thoroughness

Buyers will notice dirt that you have become blind to. As a homeowner, you've become comfortable living with a certain amount of your own dirt—I know it sounds gross, but it's true. When it comes to selling a home, you need to put yourself in the shoes of a picky buyer and view your home critically. Nothing is more off-putting than someone else's dirt. Thoroughly clean your home—literally from top to bottom!

Don't Forget Your Windows

Cleaning Tip!

Start deep cleaning after your repairs and updates are completed. Otherwise, all your hard work will be ruined by dirty work boots and construction dust.

Window cleaning is something that is often neglected by homeowners until they put their home up for sale. If you haven't had your windows cleaned in the past year, clean them shortly before you put your home on the market. It can make a surprising difference in both the amount of light

and the quality of the light that comes in your home—and it just makes the whole place feel cleaner. This is a task that a lot of home sellers hire a professional to do, but if you're able to do it yourself, you will save some money that way.

Cleaning Your Home's Exterior

The outside of your home probably needs cleaning too. Power-washing exterior walls, decks, patios, porches, stairs, roofs, and outdoor furniture can be a good idea for any areas that have a build-up of moss and algae or dirt, and it will give your home a fresh new look to boost its curb appeal. Clean doors, areas around doors, and lighting. Remove old plant pots and broken items, and put away toys, garden equipment, and trash cans.

Top Five Places People Forget to Clean

1. Interior doors and door frames
2. Light switches
3. Bathroom ceilings and exhaust fan
4. Ceiling corners
5. Light fixtures and ceiling fans

Odors

It's very difficult for anyone to detect odors in their own home. Ask a friend, relative, real estate agent, or stager to give you an honest assessment of the odors in yours. If you need to do some odor remediation, invite them back when you think you've got the problem solved to see if you've been successful.

SOLUTIONS TO SOME COMMON ODOR PROBLEMS

Cigarette Smoke

- Clean out ashtrays, open windows often, turn on fans.
- Sprinkle baking soda on wall-to-wall carpeting and furniture, let sit for at least twenty-four hours, then vacuum—better still, remove carpeting from the home.
- Remove all drapery, cushions, area rugs, throws, and bed linens.
- Wash walls and hard surfaces with a combination of water and white vinegar.
- Replace furnace filter, vacuum air ducts, clean your air conditioners.
- Smoke outside, away from open windows.

Mold and Mildew

- Remove any items that may be damp and causing odors, such as cardboard boxes, towels, clothes, or other porous materials.
- In areas with visible mildew, scrub with a combination of bleach and water (or undiluted white vinegar), then rinse with plain water.
- Always use a mask when working with mold or mildew.

Cat Urine

- Cat urine can be so strong and off-putting, it gets its own category here.
- Remove furniture and rugs that have been soiled.
- Use an enzyme-based product on anything that can't be removed.
- Scoop litter boxes *every* day and replace litter at least once a week—more often when you are having showings.

Masking Odors

A lot of people don't like the artificial scents used in most air fresheners, so don't use them. Here are some alternatives to try:

- Use coffee grounds as mulch for your indoor plant containers. It will make your home smell good and be good for your plants too!

- Soak cotton balls or small cotton rags with vanilla extract or essential oils and place in hidden places around your home.
- Make an essential oil spritzer from an old spray bottle filled with a combination of vodka or rubbing alcohol, water, and essential oil. Spray on furniture and other porous materials.

Pets

Pets should be neither seen, heard, nor smelled during a home viewing. The ideal thing to do is to find another place for your pets to stay while your house is on the market.

If your pet must live with you during this time, here some important things you need to do:

- Remove your pets during showings.
- Designate a closet or cupboard to hide your pet's bowls, beds, crates, cages, tanks, scratching posts, feeders, leashes, toys, etc., during showings.
- Move litter boxes to an inconspicuous place and clean them daily.
- Poop-scoop your lawn.
- Vacuum pet fur often.

Cleaning Tip!

Different floors need different cleaning methods.

- Polyurethaned hardwood: A very small amount of soapy water, then dry after with a towel.
- Waxed or untreated wood: No liquid ever—just vacuum and spot-clean, first with a moist towel, and then immediately with a dry towel.
- Tile, vinyl, and cork: A vinegar-based cleaner; be careful with cork not to use much liquid.
- Unsealed stone: Water only or a steamer.
- Sealed stone, linoleum, and laminates: Soapy water. Be careful with laminates not to use much liquid; it will get through the cracks and ruin the laminat .
- Carpet: rent a steamer or hire a pro for a thorough clean.

Cleaning Checklist

FOYER/ENTRANCE

- Look up in the ceiling corners; clean any cobwebs.
- Keep looking up, this time at the light fixture—clean it.
- Clean the front door (both sides) as well as the door frame.
- Clean the light switches and switch plates.
- Clean the tops of artwork and mirrors.
- Clean the walls (or repaint if necessary).
- Clean the baseboards and the trim around windows and doors.
- Clean the floor; get in the corners.
- Clean inside the closet, top to bottom.
- Clean furniture.
- Clean area rugs.
- Clean windows.

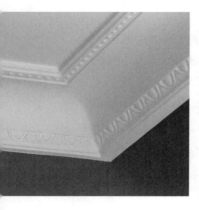

LIVING ROOM

- Clean light fixtures.
- Clean ceiling corners.
- Clean light switches and switch plates.
- Clean the tops of artwork and mirrors.
- Clean walls (or repaint if necessary).
- Clean baseboards and trim around windows and doors.
- Clean the floor; get in the corners.
- Clean furniture.
- Clean area rugs.
- Clean fireplace (if applicable).
- Clean windows.

DINING ROOM

- Clean light fixtures.
- Clean ceiling corners.
- Clean the light switches and switch plates.
- Clean the tops of artwork and mirrors.
- Clean the walls (or repaint if necessary).
- Clean the baseboards and the trim around windows and doors.
- Clean the floor; get in the corners.
- Clean furniture.
- Clean area rugs.
- Clean windows.

Make Your Own Cleaning Solutions!

They're better for the environment, and they're healthier for you too. Make them inside your empty store-bought spray bottles that will already be labeled "all-purpose cleaner" or "glass cleaner" so you'll always know what's inside.

All-Purpose Cleaner

- ½ cup white vinegar
- 2 cups water
- 1 tablespoon dish soap
- 20 drops essential oil (optional)

Glass Cleaner

- ½ cup white vinegar
- 2 cups water
- ¼ cup rubbing alcohol

KITCHEN

- Clean inside of kitchen cabinets and drawers.
- Clean inside and outside of fridge, stove, microwave, and any other appliances.
- Clean cabinet doors and drawer fronts, especially around drawer handles, the stove, and the sink.
- Clean under the sink.
- Clean light switches.
- Clean light fixtures.
- Clean baseboards.
- Clean floors.
- Clean exhaust unit over stove.
- Clean light fixtures.
- Clean ceiling corners.

- Clean the light switches and switch plates.
- Clean the tops of artwork and mirrors.
- Clean the walls (or repaint if necessary).
- Clean the baseboards and trim around windows and doors.
- Clean the floor; get in the corners.
- Clean furniture.
- Clean area rugs.
- Clean windows.

FAMILY ROOMS, REC ROOMS, MEDIA ROOMS, AND OTHER RECREATIONAL INDOOR SPACES

- Clean media stand.
- Clean video and audio equipment and speakers.
- Clean game tables and exercise equipment.
- Clean light fixtures.
- Clean ceiling corners.
- Clean the light switches and switch plates.
- Clean the tops of artwork and mirrors.
- Clean the walls (or repaint if necessary).
- Clean the baseboards and trim around windows and doors.
- Clean the floor; get in the corners.
- Clean furniture.
- Clean area rugs.
- Clean fireplace (if applicable).
- Clean windows.

Cleaning Tip!

Some buyers will be taller or shorter than you are. Stand on a chair and see what taller people see. Then crouch down and see what shorter people and those in wheelchairs might see. You may notice some areas that haven't been cleaned—ever!!

OFFICE

- Clean computer, printer, and other office equipment.
- Clean light fixtures.
- Clean ceiling corners.
- Clean the light switches and switch plates.
- Clean the tops of artwork and mirrors.
- Clean the walls (or repaint if necessary).
- Clean the baseboards, and trim around windows and doors.
- Clean the floor; get in the corners.
- Clean furniture.
- Clean area rugs.
- Clean windows.

BEDROOMS

- Clean existing bed linens or add new.
- Clean light fixtures.
- Clean ceiling corners.
- Clean the light switches and switch plates.
- Clean the tops of artwork and mirrors.
- Clean the walls (or repaint if necessary).
- Clean the baseboards, and trim around windows and doors.
- Clean closet.
- Clean the floor; get in the corners.
- Clean furniture.
- Clean area rugs.
- Clean windows.

BATHROOMS

- Clean inside and outside of vanity and medicine cabinets.
- Clean any open shelving.
- Clean all tiles, shower area, and the tub.
- Clean grout and caulking.
- Clean shower curtain or replace.
- Clean toilet.
- Clean light fixtures.
- Clean condensation build-up from ceiling.
- Clean the light switches and switch plates.
- Clean the tops of artwork and mirrors.
- Clean the walls (or repaint if necessary).
- Clean the baseboards, and trim around windows and doors.
- Clean the floor; get in the corners.
- Clean windows.

LAUNDRY AREA

- Clean inside and outside of washer and dryer.
- Clean any open shelving.
- Clean sink.
- Clean light fixtures.
- Clean the light switches and switch plates.
- Clean the tops of artwork and mirrors.
- Clean the walls (or repaint if necessary).
- Clean the baseboards, and trim around windows and doors.
- Clean the floor; get in the corners.
- Clean windows.

ATTICS, GARAGES, STORAGE ROOMS

- Clean any open shelving.
- Clean light fixtures.
- Clean the light switches and switch plates.
- Clean the walls (or repaint if necessary).
- Clean the baseboards and trim around windows and doors.
- Clean the floor; get in the corners.
- Clean windows.

OUTSIDE

- Clean front door and area around it.
- Clean exterior lights.
- Power-wash algae and mold from exterior walls, roof, porch, stairs, patio, deck, outdoor furniture.
- Remove fallen leaves, branches and twigs.
- Clean windows.

Summary

- Buyers love clean homes, so make yours the cleanest it's ever been.
- Cleaning can cost you nothing but result in a higher, quicker sale.
- Remove odors before you go on the market.
- Pets require extra cleaning and should be removed during showings.

Step Six:
Style to Sell

Time to Style!

Now for the step that most people associate with the term "home staging"! For a lot of people, this is the fun part—an opportunity to play with the furniture, accessories, and artwork. For others, this step is intimidating or an annoyance. Either way, the following styling tips will help you sell your home.

It's the styling that makes all the difference and turns an "okay" house to a "wow" house. Smart styling will make your home feel larger and brighter, highlight selling features, and cause buyers to fall head over heels in love with your home. If you're hiring a home stager, this might be where they come in to work their magic. They may have already given you advice on repairs, updates, depersonalizing, decluttering, and cleaning, and now's the time when they step in to style your home for maximum buyer appeal.

But, as powerful as styling is, don't think that the previous chapters about staging aren't all that important, because they are. If you haven't done the first five steps of successful home staging, then you're not going to achieve the top-dollar price that you're after. None of the following advice, tips, and tricks are going to help sell your home if it is cluttered, full of personal items, dirty, outdated, and in need of repairs.

Common Interior Styles

First, let's talk about determining a style for your staging. There are many different interior design and decorating styles, and they apply to home staging too. What is the architectural style of your home? You can work with that as a foundation, but you can add other elements as well. Remember your target buyer and the styles they prefer. If you are surveying your own furniture and accessories and determining which items to use for your staging, look for the styles that are on trend and popular with buyers—use those for the staging and pack the rest for storage while you are on the market.

Here are a few of the most common styles:

1. Traditional: Rolled-arm sofas, Persian rugs, generous curtains, polished antiques, dark woods, ornate fabrics, and detailing.

2. Modern: Smooth and sleek with little décor. Simple lines, nothing ornate or detailed. Metals and shiny surfaces, mostly neutral colors.

3. Transitional: In between traditional and modern. A very common style that is less ornate and heavy than traditional, but more comfy and detailed than modern.

4. Mid-Century Modern: Originated in the 1950s. Features long, low, simple lines and simplicity in form and function. Brings the outside in, with large windows, teak and walnut wood, and other natural elements. Often features Scandinavian mid-century furniture.

5. Farmhouse: Transitional style with rustic accents. Modern Farmhouse is an updated version with lots of neutral colors and natural accents, sometimes incorporating industrial elements.

6. Boho: An eclectic mix of patterns, styles, layers, and textures, often incorporating vintage and rustic elements.

7. Scandinavian: An understated look with simple lines, light woods, light walls, natural elements, slightly minimalist, sometimes with pops of color.

8. Industrial: Open loft look with distressed woods and metals, exposed brick, stainless steel, factory and restaurant-kitchen detailing.

Traditional style.

Transitional style.

Modern style.

What Is the Best Style for Your Home?

Transitional is one of the most common styles used for staging, since it appeals to the widest group of buyers. For the majority of homes and markets, transitional works best for home staging. But there are exceptions.

When determining the style that is right for your home staging, you need to ask yourself two questions. What look is trending for your target buyer? And what is the architectural style of your home?

If your home's architectural style is currently on trend with buyers, use the same style for the furniture and accessories—that way you will be highlighting your home's style, which may be its biggest selling feature. For example, if mid-century modern homes are in demand in your area and you have a mid-century modern home, staging with mid-century furniture and accessories will draw those buyers in from far and wide.

If your home's style isn't currently on trend with buyers, then it would be best to go with a transitional look which works in almost any home. For example, if your home is very traditional and that style isn't currently popular with buyers, using a transitional style will give it a less traditional feel and appeal to more buyers. But it's not necessary to stick completely with one style or another. Most homes are a mixture. Very often, staged homes are mostly transitional with current on-trend elements added.

This traditional home has been updated by painting the cabinets and woodwork a soft white and using a lighter—less heavy—color palette.

Color Flow Throughout the Home

A light neutral color palette is generally the best bet for staging, with darks added for drama and contrast, along with plenty of natural elements for texture. But it is also a common staging practice to use an accent color or two, if they are on trend and appeal to most buyers in a particular market. Be sure that you aren't using outdated colors. Talk to a stager about current trends, or do your own research on what is trending, before you commit to using colors in staging.

Use the same color palette throughout the home. It gives the buyer a great feeling to walk through a home with a cohesive color palette. It has a calming effect and makes the home feel well-designed, professional, and unified. And it allows energy to flow easily from one room to another. Using colors from different palettes in each room has a jarring effect and feels disjointed.

However, it's not problematic to use different accent colors in the bedrooms, especially if they are on a separate floor from the rest of the home. In children's bedrooms, you may want to use more color. And in primary bedrooms, calm, soothing colors are ideal.

The Secret of Styling to Sell: Contrast

Contrast commands attention and turns a boring space into a vibrant one. An all-white room with a white rug, white furniture, or white counters and cabinets will look light and bright—but, without contrast, it won't have any life. So how do you achieve contrast in a white room and still maintain a beautiful, bright look? By adding wood elements, natural fibers, dark accents, and greenery. On the flip side, if your room is all dark and moody, then add lots of light accents for contrast, along with wood, natural fibers, and greenery. Adding color is another way to achieve contrast, but when staging, keep your colors to a minimum.

Balance and Repetition

Colors, tones, and textures work best when they are repeated a few times and positioned so that they are balanced around a room. If you have a room that is mostly neutral colors, but you have an accent color, that color should appear several times, in different parts of the room. Let's say your accent color is yellow. You don't want all of your yellow accents in one corner. Spread them out so that the room feels more balanced.

If you have metal or natural wood elements, they should be repeated as well, in several points in the room. Same with lights and darks. You don't want all of the dark items on one side, and the light items on the other.

In this living room, several elements are balanced and repeated in different parts of the room: the color blue, the fluffy white texture, wood tones, and dark gray/black.

Where Is Your Focal Point?

A focal point is the place where a viewer's eye will be first drawn. Every room needs a focal point; it's often what the rest of the room will be designed around. It's ideal if your focal point is also a selling feature, since your goal is to highlight your selling features so that buyers are sure to notice them.

Your focal point should be seen from the entrance to the room. If a room has more than one entrance, the focal point should be seen directly from the entrance most likely to be used by the buyer the first time they enter the room. Depending on the room, a focal point might be a fireplace, a view, a bed, a dining table, a piece of artwork, or a grouping of furniture, artwork, and accessories.

By centering the furniture around the fireplace which is the focal point of the room, the eye is drawn to it and buyers can't help but notice this beautiful selling feature.

There are several ways that you can draw the eye to your focal point. To illustrate how you might use each method, let me talk you through an example. Let's say you have a black stone fireplace with an exposed wood mantel. What can you do to draw attention to it?

1. *Contrast.* Contrasting tones or colors attract our attention. To contrast the black stone, you could place thick white pillar candles on the mantel, which would contrast with the black stone behind them.

2. *Color.* Pops of color also command attention, especially if they are surrounded by neutrals. So if you placed some greenery on that mantel beside the white candles, the bright green would also draw the eye.

3. *Shine.* Metals and mirrors catch the eye as well. So maybe you hang a metal-framed mirror over the mantel to add some bling.

4. *Lighting.* To complete our example, I would add some overhead directional lighting that is pointed toward the fireplace.

Perfect—the fireplace is now styled to create a focal point and draw attention to it as a selling feature.

Start with your focal point, style it first, and then style the rest of the room when you're sure that you have that working. In order to keep the attention to the focal point, don't have a lot of competing contrast in the room; otherwise the eye will be drawn all over the place. Keep it simple.

How to Design a Room Around an Anchor Piece

An easy trick to achieving a coherently designed room is to start with one item and "build" the design of the room around it. When you start with one item and base your design choices on it, you don't wind up with conflicting color schemes or styles, and everything will more effortlessly tie together. Some common things that might be used as anchor pieces are artwork, a throw pillow, or a piece of furniture. The anchor piece will be the inspiration for the color, pattern, and texture choices in the rest of the room.

Here are two examples of how one item can be used to anchor the rest of the design choices in a room:

Artwork in a Living Room.

In this example, let's imagine you're going to hang some artwork on a wall over a light, neutral-colored sofa that is the focal point of your living room. Choose a piece of artwork that you want to use as your anchor piece. Then pick a color from that artwork and use it in several other places in the room. Keep in mind that in staging, you want to use mostly neutrals, so don't go crazy with the color. But as an example, if the artwork has some navy in it, then you could add navy throw pillows to the light neutral sofa below it. Then add an art book with a navy cover on the coffee table beside a beautiful sculptural object, and a navy vase with greenery on a console table on the other side of the room. Whenever you're considering whether an item works in the room, refer to the anchor piece and see if it works with that. If it does, it should look great in the room. Artwork makes a fabulous anchor piece in almost any room, especially when it is the focal point.

Throw Pillow in a Bedroom.

In this example, a bed covered with white bed linens and a throw pillow in the center is the focal point. Choose a throw pillow that contrasts with the white bedding to use as the anchor piece. Then select a color or texture in the pillow and repeat it in other places in the room. Let's say your throw pillow is dark gray velvet with silver embroidery. Place a matching gray throw blanket, folded, at the end of the bed and a dark gray and white rug for the floor. Add silver-colored matching bedside lamps, a silver vase with some flowers on the dresser, and a mirror with a silver frame over the bed. Voila! A simple, cohesive design.

Before and after example of a living room in an "occupied" staging which utilized the artwork over the sofa as an anchor piece: The light turquoise in the artwork was repeated in the accessories, the silver on the frame was repeated in the lighting, and the white of the artwork mat was repeated in the white rug which helped to brighten up the room.

The Most Important Design Tip You Need to Know for Staging

Pay attention, because this might actually be the most important tip in this whole book. So, if you're skimming through the book and you've got this far, slow down and make sure you read this next tip. If you remember one thing from this book, remember this, and home room design will improve dramatically.

But first, think about this: where should you stand when you're trying to make a room look nice? It may sound like a crazy question, like, why would it matter where you stand? But just think: You're trying to create something that is pleasing to the eye. So where does the eye see it? When you paint a painting, it's two-dimensional and it's obvious that you stand in front of a painting and view it from there. And when you create a sculpture, it's three-dimensional, so you probably want it to look good from all perspectives. With both of these situations, you're seeing the object from a minimum of a few feet away. But with a room, you're standing *in* it while you're styling it. How can you tell how good it looks if you're standing inside it? You can't.

So here's the tip: Stand outside the room and look at it from the main entrance to the room. That is the viewpoint that is the most important. You need to get out of the room and look at it from a distance to really see if it is working or not. Buyers will see it from that vantage point, and that's where they will form their first impression—and it will be a lasting impression. If a buyer thinks your living room looks gorgeous as they walk into the room, they will remember it that way as they walk out—and how that is how they will describe it to their friends and family.

So let's say you're standing just outside the room, looking in. What should you be looking for? What you need to do is ask yourself these questions:

- Does the room (or any part of it) look crowded?
- Are the selling features of the room plainly evident from that vantage point?
- Does the arrangement of the furniture invite you to walk straight in, or is your path blocked?
- How does the arrangement of your accessories look from that vantage point?
- Does the room look light-filled?
- Are the colors, tones, and textures evenly spaced around the room?

Answer these questions, then move things around accordingly until you think you might have it right.

When you're assessing the overall look of a room, stand just outside the room and judge it from there. That's where buyers will first see the room—and the feeling that they get there is the most important.

And here is yet another tip: Take a photo from that vantage point outside the room. This will help you see the room differently and you will probably notice things that you hadn't noticed with the naked eye. Take a photo, make adjustments, and then take another photo to see if it looks better. Keep going until it looks great.

If your room has several entrances, start with the entrance that buyers will most likely see first and make that look great. Then move to the other entrances and see how they look from there. If your home is open concept and you have a huge multi-purpose room, view the room from the main entrance first and then from other key vantage points where buyers may pause and look around—maybe at a kitchen island, or sitting on a couch.

Also, if you happen to know where the marketing photo will be shot, that is a great place to view the room too. The marketing photo will usually include the focal point and selling features and be shot from a point far enough back that the photographer can get a good portion of the room in the shot.

The Essential Rules of Staging—That Have Nothing to Do with Design

A lot of people are intimidated by staging because they aren't confident about their design sense. Maybe they aren't sure what looks good and what doesn't. Or they know good design when they see it, but they don't know how to achieve it. While good design makes a huge difference in home staging, there are actually six very important rules to a successful home staging that have nothing to do with design at all! If you follow each of these rules, you will have gone a long way toward staging your home successfully.

RULE ONE: DETERMINE ONE PURPOSE FOR EACH ROOM

One of the most important rules of staging is to have only *one* purpose for every room. For example: In real life, primary bedrooms are often used as exercise rooms and offices—as well as bedrooms, of course. However, when staging, primary bedrooms should be shown only as bedrooms. Either find another place for that exercise equipment and desk, or put them in storage while you show your home.

Before and after photos of a family room. The family living in this house was used as a combination office, guest bedroom, and TV room. For staging purposes, we simplified it to one room: a TV room. Always consider the other rooms in the home and what buyers might be looking for. Since the living room in this house was small and formal, it made sense to show buyers a less formal space where the family could hang out.

RULE TWO: THE PURPOSE OF EACH ROOM SHOULD BE THE ONE ORIGINALLY INTENDED BY THE ARCHITECT OR DESIGNER OF THE HOME

For example, I've seen kitchen nooks used as offices, dining rooms used as music rooms, formal living rooms used as kids' playrooms, and bedrooms used as storage spaces. And that's fantastic for the homeowners, since it works for their lifestyle, but it doesn't work for staging. When staging, turn those spaces you've transformed for your specific lifestyle back into the purpose for which they were originally intended. This helps with depersonalizing the space and allows prospective buyers to more easily imagine how they would live there, which is an important step for them in the buying process.

Before and after photos of a kitchen. This breakfast nook had been converted to a home office to suit the home seller's lifestyle, but it was actually part of the kitchen. When we were hired to stage it, we converted the room back to its original purpose. This made it easier for the buyers to imagine themselves living within the home, rather than trying to look past the home seller's repurposing.

RULE THREE: HIGHLIGHT SELLING FEATURES

Draw attention to the features you want prospective buyers to notice. Be aware of your home's selling features and make sure that you're not hiding them. Remove furniture placed in front of fireplaces, take heavy drapes from large windows, and uncover your hardwood floors.

BEFORE

Before and after photos of a living room. A large sofa was completely covering the fireplace in this living room. Don't hide your home's selling features—make sure that they are obvious to prospective buyers.

AFTER

RULE FOUR: MAKE EACH ROOM APPEAR AS LARGE AS POSSIBLE

This is simple to do. Reduce the amount of furniture you normally have. You want to have less furniture in staging than you would have if you normally lived in a home. Have just enough furniture to show buyers how the space can be used and no more. If your home feels kind of empty, that's okay. With staging, less is more. Don't use oversized furniture in small or medium-sized rooms. Smaller furniture is generally better for staging. Strategically placed mirrors and less clutter also create the appearance of a larger space.

BEFORE

Before and after photos of an office niche. This office space has just enough furniture and accessories to let buyers know how this space might be used, without any crowding. It's hard for buyers to tell how much furniture can fit into an empty room. So by adding a little furniture, a room actually looks bigger with furniture than when empty.

AFTER

RULE FIVE: MAKE EACH ROOM APPEAR AS LIGHT AS POSSIBLE

Open all window treatments as much as possible. Remove any heavy curtains that cover windows (see page 83). If you don't need the window treatments for privacy, remove them completely. Paint walls light neutral colors (see page 87). Be sure that you have ample lighting for each room and that it's all in working order.

Before and after photos of child's bedroom. By removing window treatments and dark busy wallpaper, this room felt much lighter and brighter.

RULE SIX: DO NOT OBSTRUCT THE BUYERS' FLOW AS THEY WALK THROUGH YOUR HOME

Arrange furniture so that it invites buyers to walk straight into a room, rather than dodging around chairs or lamps. Don't block doors to other rooms or doors to exterior spaces. Even if you personally never use those doors, buyers may want to use the space differently than you do, so invite them to walk around by keeping all doors unobstructed.

Arrange your furniture in a way that leaves a lot of space for the buyers to walk from room to room.

Furniture for Staging

If you'll be living in your home while it is on the market, you'll need to reduce your furniture and put some in storage. But what furniture do you keep for your staging and what do you move to storage? The best thing to do is to have a staging consultation from a local stager who will make suggestions along these lines. If that is not an option for you, here are some recommendations:

1. Tag everything that you won't be using for staging. I recommend going through your home with painter's tape and tagging the furniture that you'll be moving for your staging. On the tape you can write where it is going—either to another room or to storage.

2. Reduce the amount of furniture you have in each room. Just about every house can benefit from reducing the amount of furniture for staging.

3. Avoid oversized furniture. Choose small pieces when possible. Remove tall cabinets. Remember, you want your rooms to look larger, so smaller-sized furniture is best. Oversized pieces will still work in some large, luxury homes, but if your home is average to small-sized, your space will look better with smaller furniture pieces.

Dark, patterned, oversized furniture does not work well for staging in photos or in person. Look for smaller-sized, light-colored furniture and add contrast through accent pieces and accessories.

4. Light, neutral colors are ideal. When possible, choose light neutral pieces because light colors make the room feel brighter and larger.

5. Glass-topped tables. Professional stagers love glass-topped tables and use them a *lot* because they know that they take up less visual space, thereby making a space feel larger. They also reflect light, making the room feel a little brighter.

6. Furniture with shiny metals. Items such as tables with metal bases are also used a lot by home stagers—since the metal is reflective, it adds light, and the "bling" can help a room feel more expensive.

7. Renting furniture. In a lot of locations, there are companies that rent furniture. Depending on your home's price point and the company's rental prices, it might make sense for you to rent furniture more suited for staging. Rental furniture can be an excellent way to transform a room—or several rooms. If done right, the cost of the rental furniture is surpassed by the increase in the selling price of the home.

8. Borrowing furniture. If rental furniture isn't an option for you and you feel that your home could really benefit from different furniture for your staging, think about whether you may be able to borrow some pieces from friends or family.

So the question is, where do you put the furniture that won't be used for staging? If it's just a few items, maybe you have room within your home to store it. Perhaps a garage or basement. Many people use storage units or a friend's garage. Other people are lucky enough to already have access to their new home so they do two moves: one to remove the items not needed for staging purposes, and the second one to move everything else after the house has sold.

To find out more about which furniture is best for specific rooms, turn to Chapter X.

Artwork for Staging

When you're preparing your home for sale, don't automatically leave your artwork hanging in the same place you've always had it. If you're moving your furniture to different locations, you'll probably want to move your artwork as well. And remember that, in staging, less is more. Don't feel that you need to fill every wall. You can leave some walls blank. You may just want to have artwork in the focal point of a room: over a fireplace, sofa, bed, or console table or on the wall facing the entrance to a room.

TYPES OF ARTWORK

Here are the "rules" for types of artwork to use when staging:

1. No nudes, no matter how artistic or tasteful.

2. Nothing religious. Prepack all religious items, including artwork.

3. Nothing personal. Depersonalizing was covered in detail earlier, but depersonalizing also extends to personal crafts. Large hanging quilts command attention and are therefore distracting from the house itself—and they are taste specific too, which is a staging no-no. You're selling the house, not the quilts, so prepack them. Same thing goes for framed stained-glass pieces hanging in windows. Unless you're trying to hide an ugly view, let the buyers look out the window. However, I would use crafts like these two examples if they were really on trend and appealed to the target market. If you're in doubt, prepack.

4. Size must fit the space. Try to hang larger pieces in larger places and save smaller pieces for bathrooms, hallways, or other smaller spaces. Smaller pieces of artwork don't show up well in marketing photos, so only use them if you think they are really adding to the look of the room.

5. Mirrors are great for staging. They add light and sparkle and work in so many places: over a bed, a fireplace mantel, a console table, or dresser.

6. Abstracts are good, especially in neutral colors.

7. Gallery walls. These can be okay for staging, provided that they don't have any personal photos in them. But they can be tricky to get right, so I don't recommend creating one for staging. It's better to stay simple with one strong piece.

Staging Tip!

Measure twice and hang once! But if you don't get it right the first time, don't fret, just take it down and try again. It's best to have it looking right. Potential buyers won't see the holes under the art anyway. Most people leave small nail holes in the wall when they sell, but if you do need to fill the holes after you've sold, it's just as easy to fill two holes as one.

Artwork for staging works best when it's simple and neutral—in subject matter and in color. We're not necessarily talking about quality art here. The important thing is the overall feel of the room since we're selling a home, not the artwork.

HOW TO HANG ARTWORK

The most common mistake when hanging artwork is to hang it too high. Here are some handy guidelines to follow when hanging yours.

1. *Hanging on a wall.* If artwork is hung on a wall, but not over any furniture, then the center of the artwork should be at eye level. The rule of thumb that most designers follow is to hang artwork so that the center of the piece is about 58 to 60 inches (147 to 152 cm) from the floor.

2. *Hanging over a console table or buffet.* The center of the piece should also be at eye level, but if the piece is tall and the bottom of the frame would rest on the furniture if the center was at eye height, raise the artwork so that the bottom of the frame is 6 to 8 inches (15 to 20 cm) over the furniture. The maximum width of the artwork should be two-thirds of the width of the furniture it is hung over.

3. *Hanging over a sofa.* The bottom of the frame should be 6 to 8 inches (15 to 20 cm) from the top of the sofa. Ideally the width of the artwork should be two-thirds of the width of the sofa. If you have a large sofa, try hanging two or more pieces of matching artwork side by side.

Hang artwork close to the top of your sofa. One of the most common mistakes people make is hanging their artwork too high.

4. *Hanging "like" artwork together.* Hang matching artwork pieces close together so that they feel like one unit, not disconnected from each other. The space between can be as little as 1.5 inches for small artwork to 4 inches for large pieces.

5. *Hanging over a fireplace.* Artwork, mirrors, or TVs that are hung on a fireplace with a mantel should be hung so that the bottom of the frame or screen is 4 to 6 inches from the mantel. Or, for a more casual look, artwork can be placed directly on the mantel.

Rugs for Staging

Rugs are the biggest (and often the most effective) staging accessory. Changing your rugs can make a *huge* difference in how your rooms look in photos and in the overall look and feel of your room—and are the quickest way to make big changes.

RUGS ARE A POWERFUL STAGING TOOL

Because they are often the biggest item in the room, the whole personality of a room can change just by adding or changing a rug. You should always consider them when you stage your home. Purchasing some new rugs can be a really smart way to make big changes for relatively little money.

Here are just a few examples that show how useful area rugs can be when staging:

- Add a soft rug to warm up a room with tile flooring.
- Define separate living areas in an open concept floor plan with a separate rug for each area.
- Lighten up a dark room with a light rug.
- Layer area rugs on wall-to-wall carpeting to create an updated look—or hide stains.
- Freshen up a room by removing existing worn or stained area rugs and replacing with clean new ones.
- Add a cute children's rug to an unused area to suggest a kid's play space.

Open concept spaces need to have areas within the space defined, according to their use. By placing one rug in the living area and another in the dining area, the rugs in this space show buyers how they may use the space and allow them to view the space as two distinct living areas rather than one.

WHAT KINDS OF RUGS ARE BEST FOR STAGING?

Light and simple is the key! White or cream are the best colors. Very plain rugs or those with simple graphics work great for staging. They look better in photos online and are neutral enough to work with any style of home or furniture.

A plain white or light-colored or rug may seem boring or impractical, but it's a stager's best friend. They lighten up any room, make it feel clean and fresh, and provide a blank canvas for the furniture to be placed on top. And they look great in online photos. Sometimes a light, neutral-colored rug with a simple graphic design like the one below can also work well.

Natural-fiber rugs, such as sisal, jute, and seagrass, can also work well for staging. Their simplicity and warmth work well both online and in person. They can be placed in foyers, dining rooms, sunrooms, and casual sitting areas.

Staging Tip!

Consider buying new rugs to stage your home—they can make a big difference. But don't spend a lot of money on them unless you're sure you'll use them in your new home.

Money-Saving Tip!

If your current rug isn't staging-friendly but your floor looks great, prepack your rug and leave your floor without a rug at all. It's best to show off your beautiful floor to buyers.

A foolproof staging rug is white or cream-colored, either solid or lightly patterned. These rugs brighten up every room, go with everything, and look great in online photos.

WHAT KINDS OF RUGS ARE WORST FOR STAGING?

Dark patterned or ornate rugs, no matter how high the quality or how much they are worth, are not good for staging. They feel cluttered in online photos and make the room look darker. They can be very nice when you're living in a home, but when you're staging your home, roll them up and store them till you're in your new place.

Accessories for Staging

Sometimes adding a few updated accessories is all you need to do to freshen up a room. Once you know who your target buyer is, you can easily update your space by buying a few accessories that will appeal to them. It shouldn't cost you much, and it will really help buyers imagine themselves in your space. You may find that you really end up liking your new look. Most people do and are eager to incorporate some of their new staging items in their new home when they move.

There are so many, how do you choose what works in your home? There are two main factors to consider: size and color.

ACCESSORY SIZES

Accessories used for staging work best when they're medium- to large-sized. A general rule of thumb is melon-sized or larger. Small accessories aren't ideal for staging, since they don't show well in online photos and tend to clutter the photo. Larger accessories show up better in the photos and make a home feel more expensive. Even when viewed in person, a minimal number of medium-to-large accessories feels cleaner, less cluttered, and more luxurious.

ACCESSORY COLORS

Neutral colors, metals, and natural materials are best. If there is a hot on-trend color that would work in your space, then that is a good option too. The color and shade of your accessories helps determine where they should be placed. You generally want the accessory to contrast with what is behind it. For instance, if you put a white accessory on a white shelf that has a white wall behind it, that accessory will get lost. Instead, a dark or colorful accessory, something metallic, or a plant should be placed in that white environment. The opposite is also true— when staging a shelf with a dark-colored background, you don't want to put a dark-colored accessory on the shelf. Try a light-colored one, a shiny light metallic, or some greenery.

Decorative Objects

There are an infinite number of accessories that you can use for styling and a million ways to use them. Here are a few to get you started:

Trays: Trays are so useful! Use them to hold all of the other accessories together. When you're styling a space and it just won't work, try a tray to hold things together.

Baskets: Tall, vase-shaped baskets, wide, low, tray-shaped baskets, baskets to hold things, baskets to fill spaces, baskets to add texture—baskets are endlessly useful.

Sculptural Objects: Use sculptural pieces to add visual interest, interesting shapes and textures, and create a more expensive feel.

Ornamental balls: (wood, greenery or metal): Use a bunch of smaller ornamental balls to fill a large bowl, or larger ones on their own.

Art books: Stack several art books on open shelving, a few on a coffee table, or leave one open. Choose your art books based on how their subjects tie to your home, and by the colors of the covers and spines and how they tie in with your color palette.

Vases: Use vases on their own as sculptural objects on an open shelf or fill them with greenery or a fresh bouquet of flowers and place on a dining table or coffee table.

Candles: Candles add height and invoke the cozy "hygge" feeling that we all want our home to have.

Fake fruit: Faux lemons or limes are classic staging accessories. A good fake should look indistinguishable from the real thing, and the bold pop of color will add life to any kitchen.

Decorative boxes: Decorative boxes made from metal or wood add color and texture and can be especially useful when styling open shelving.

Money-Saving Tip!

Do some accessory "shopping" in your own home. Gather together all the medium-to-large accessories in your house on one large surface (maybe your dining room table or the floor in a low-traffic area). Once you have your furniture edited and placed in staging-friendly places, go to your accessory "store" and shop for the accessory that works best for each space. Don't be afraid to try things in different rooms than where you originally had them.

Use a tray to corral several items together for a more professional look.

Antique artifacts: Items like old typewriters, cameras, and small framed art provide visual interest and add character when a home is feeling too bland and sterile.

Houseplants and Flowers

Houseplants are nice to live with and are also the most fabulous staging accessory. I highly recommend having at least one form of greenery in each room. Sometimes a room can feel a little cold or uninviting, but then a house plant is added and the room magically feels better!

Faux plants have come a long way, and some look almost identical to real plants. And in online photos you definitely can't tell the difference. If you don't have a green thumb or will be away when your home is on the market, faux plants are a great option. When selecting your faux plants, choose the ones that are the most real-looking. Stores tend to carry more in the spring, so that's a good time to stock up on them. You'll have the best selection and get the best prices.

If you are using real plants, make sure they are in good condition. Don't crowd the room with too many plants. As with anything else in staging, less is more.

Here are some common situations where plants are used for staging inside homes:

- A real plant with a nice fragrant flower by the front door to welcome buyers
- Orchids and/or succulents on bathroom counters and tub surrounds
- A medium-to-large vase of flowers on a dining table, coffee table, or console table
- A small vase of flowers or greenery on a bedside table or dresser
- Potted herbs on a kitchen window or shelf

Throw Pillows

Throw pillows are fun to work with and come in so many styles and colors. They are an effective and fun way to add contrast, style, texture, and color and a great way to update as well. If you haven't updated your throw pillows in the past couple of years, they are probably looking a little tired and worn, so now is the perfect time to get some new ones. Just by adding a few updated throw pillows, the whole room can feel fresher.

An easy way to appeal to your target buyer is to think about what stores they would shop at and buy your new throw pillows there. That's right, throw pillows can be a marketing tool when it comes to staging. When you update in a way that appeals to buyers, you're helping them imagine themselves in the space and feel at home. And when buyers feel at home, they are more likely to make an offer on yours!

But there are so many styles and colors of throw pillows to choose from, so how do you decide which to choose? Here are some guidelines:

1. Be sure that the pillow contrasts with what it is placed against. If you place a dark pillow on a dark sofa, the pillow will have no visual impact and will get lost. So if you have a dark sofa, choose light or medium-toned pillows. Either solid cream or white, or ones with a cream or white background, are good for staging on a dark sofa. That way the pillows will pop from the sofa—and add some lightness to the room.

Light throw pillows work best on dark sofas.

2. If you have a white or very light sofa, then go the opposite direction. Some medium-toned or darker throw pillows can be used to pop against the light color of the sofa.

3. If you're choosing throw pillows that have a pattern, go with a pattern that is bold. Delicate, detailed patterns don't show up well in the marketing photos.

4. The colors of throw pillows should either be neutral or tie in with your home's color story (see page 87).

Throws

Throws (or small blankets) are used in much the same way throw pillows are used—to provide contrast and interest in the room. They can be used at the foot of a bed, draped carefully over a chair, or on a sofa. You can either fold them into a perfect rectangle or drape them casually. Ironically, it is often harder to get a nice casual drape than to fold them perfectly.

Staging Tips—Room by Room

Now that you've got the basics of styling, you're ready for more specific information on each room in your home. While every room in every home is different, there are some common ways to style each room and things to keep in mind. Here are some tips and tricks to help you style each room.

FOYERS AND ENTRANCES

Buyers make up their mind whether they like a house within the first seven seconds of entering a home! So keep this in mind and be sure that your prospective buyers feel welcomed by what they see immediately as they walk in the door.

First, be sure you've done a thorough job with your repairs, updates, decluttering, and depersonalizing. Have you removed any key racks, boot trays, shoe racks, umbrella holders, mail caddies, and worn welcome mats? If so, here are some effective ways to stage your foyer.

Styling Tip!

Because you'll have less furniture and accessories when staging, there will be less to visually compete for your attention and each piece will get noticed. So make sure it works to earn its place in the room.

Using a Console Table with a Wall Mirror

This is probably the most common and most effective way to stage a foyer. Console tables are narrow, low-profile tables that are often placed near front doors. Homeowners find them handy because they provide a place to drop keys, bags, or other miscellaneous items. They are also a favorite with home stagers, but for different reasons:

- They are narrow and don't take up a lot of floor space, so they help the room look big (remember, you want small-scale furniture when staging).

- They provide a horizontal place to put something attractive to greet buyers when they come in. Flowers or other plants, accessories, and lamps are often used to create a good first impression.

- The wall space above a console table can be used to hang a mirror, which provides reflective light (remember, you want a lot of light) or attractive artwork.

- They act as a focal point.

- They are often also used by real estate agents to place sell sheets or reminders for people to remove their shoes or put on shoe protectors.

A mirror hung on the wall above a console table is an effective and classic way to stage a foyer. When hanging your mirror or artwork, be sure you don't hang it too high. Remember that you want the artwork to be hung so that the center is about eye height. It should visually tie in with the console and the accessories, not float way up above them.

Other Foyer Staging Solutions

Large formal foyers with grand staircases often benefit from a round table with a tall vase of flowers or greenery. Narrow or small entrance halls should not be crowded with furniture at all—a nice piece of artwork or a mirror, and possibly an attractive rug, are enough.

If you have wall hooks by your front door, they should be styled simply. Choose one nice coat or sweater in a color that ties in with the color theme of your home. You can add more whimsical elements, like a basket, hat, or umbrella, as well. Or be strategic and hang items that will remind buyers of the fun things to do in your area. For instance, if the home you're selling is near a beach, you could have an attractive straw tote bag with rolled towels (in colors that coordinate with your color scheme or in neutrals). If you have a free-standing coat rack, remove it. They tend to look cluttered, and it's better to store your coats elsewhere while staging.

A more informal way to style a foyer is with a bench and a throw pillow or two.

Staging Tip!

Choose a fragrant plant to put near the entrance to your home. A small one can sit on a console table, or if it's larger, place it in a nearby corner.

Before you finish styling this room, go outside your home and come back through the door, imagining yourself as a prospective buyer. Stand there for a few minutes. Look straight ahead, look up, and look down. What do you see? Take a deep breath. What do you smell? If anything needs adjusting, do it now.

If you don't have a separate entrance space or hall at all and your front door opens directly into your living room, take out any entry-type furniture and accessories. Remember Rule Number One: One purpose for each room. It's better not to crowd the space with two purposes, so style it solely as a living room.

LIVING ROOMS

After your foyer, your living room is often one of the first rooms that buyers will see. Since it is usually a key room, it is worth staging properly. Once you've done any needed repairs or painting and you've decluttered and depersonalized and deep cleaned, you're ready to maximize its appeal to buyers.

No two houses are the same, and each homeowner is starting with different furniture and accessories, so there is no cookie-cutter solution that works for every living room, but here are some guidelines that work for most living rooms and some pointers on showing your living room so that it "wows" buyers as soon as they see it.

Highlight Selling Features

Your first task in staging your living room is to focus on any specific selling features to highlight. Here are some common living room selling features and how to stage them.

Fireplace: Fireplaces are a great living room selling feature. They appeal to buyers, and they act as a focal point for your furniture. Be sure your fireplace is cleaned out and then, if it is a traditional wood-burning fireplace, signal this feature to buyers by placing some logs on the fireplace grate and possibly some in a basket beside the fireplace as well. Silver birch logs are perfect for this. Hang a large mirror or piece of artwork over the mantel and place a medium- or large-sized accessory on either side of the mirror or artwork. If you are aiming for a more formal look, the accessories should be matching. For a more informal look, choose non-matching items.

High Ceilings: To call attention to your high ceilings, you want to pull the buyer's eye up as they enter the room. Do this by adding something with contrast in a high space, such as large artwork or stacking matching art pieces. Or hang a chandelier that contrasts with the wall colors and catches the eye.

Styling Tip!

Style hooks simply and stylishly. When in doubt, leave them empty.

Large Rooms: To take full advantage of any large rooms, stage the foreground of the room (the part closest to the room's entrance) with low-contrast neutrals and have something with high contrast or bold color at the far end of the room. This will pull the buyer's eye immediately to the far end of the room and emphasize its size.

Hardwood or other desired floors: Keep them mostly exposed so that they show prominently in online photos.

Built-in Shelving: Style the shelving with just a few medium-to-large items that contrast the color of the shelving, and add some shiny items and some greenery. The contrast and the greenery will draw the buyer's eye when they enter the room. Small accessories feel like clutter when staging, especially in photos, so choose larger items that read well from a distance. Read more about styling open shelving on page 184.

Focal Point

Earlier in this chapter, we touched on the importance of styling around a focal point. If there is a fireplace or other selling feature on the wall that you see as you enter your living room, then that selling feature should be your focal point. If you don't have any architectural or selling features to highlight on that wall, that's okay, you can create a focal point. You can do this easily by placing a nice piece of artwork on this wall with a sofa under it and building a conversation group of furniture around that as outlined on page 182.

A TV is not a good focal point for a living room (although it would work in a den or media room), so if you have a TV on your living room focal wall, you should move it. I know that, if your TV is wall mounted and hardwired, it can be difficult to move and will involve patching and painting the wall once you've taken it down. But it is worth doing. You don't want a huge TV to be the first thing buyers are going to see when they come into your living room. It's best to move the TV to a different room, a different wall, or even better, prepack it for your next place and do without it for a while. One exception: if your TV is over your fireplace and the fireplace is your focal point, that's okay. That works, because the fireplace is the selling point and you're bringing attention to it. In that case, place accessories on the mantel on either side of the TV.

Did You Know?

The most common rooms to stage are the living room (93 percent), the kitchen (84 percent), the master bedroom (78 percent), and the dining room (72 percent).

Source: 2019 Profile of Home Staging, National Association of REALTORS® Research Group.

The furniture in this living room is arranged to create a conversation group and is centered around the fireplace which is the focal point of the room. It is also arranged in a way that invites the buyer in and does not obstruct their path into the space.

Placing the Furniture

A living room should be an inviting place to relax and entertain. But don't just line the furniture up all along the walls. Create a conversation group with your furniture centered around your focal point. What is a conversation group? Literally imagine that a number of people are sitting in your furniture, having a conversation. Are those people close enough to hear each other without raising their voices? Can they see each other without turning at an uncomfortable angle? If the answer is yes—then you have a nice conversation group. A common way to create a conversation group is to place the furniture around a coffee table with a large rug underneath.

Remember Rule 6: Do not obstruct the buyer's flow (page 167). In a living room, this means arranging the furniture in a way that invites the buyers into the heart of the room. Try not to have the backs of any furniture facing the buyer as they walk in the room. Also, don't crowd the furniture, and make sure you leave plenty of room for the buyers to come straight in and sit on a sofa or comfy chair. A good rule of thumb is to leave a path at least at three feet wide—any less than that and it will feel tight and crowded. Even if buyers are not actually going to hang out on your furniture, you want them to feel encouraged to do so.

And don't forget Step Four: Declutter your room by simplifying and reducing the number of furniture pieces. Always remember that in staging, less is more. When you stage your home, you want to have less furniture and accessories in your home than you do when you are living in it. By removing extraneous pieces of furniture, your room will look larger and more inviting.

Living Room Area Rugs

Think of an area rug as a frame that holds the furniture in a room together. One of the biggest mistakes people make is buying rugs that are too small. Ideally, all of the furniture in your conversation group should be either fully or partially on the rug. Here is how to size your rug and how to place the furniture.

Example One: Rug too small.

Example Two: A rug that fits with the front legs on the rug.

Example Three: A rug that fits with all of the legs on the rug.

For home staging, if the living room has nice wood floors, Example Two works best, since it leaves more of a selling feature exposed. If the floor is tile, then Example Three is best, since the larger rug warms up the space more and the room feels cozier. Or, if the floors are damaged or not attractive (for instance wall-to-wall carpeting), then Example Three works best. And yes, you can layer area rugs over wall-to-wall carpeting.

Making a small investment in a new, inexpensive area rug can be a really smart way to make a big change in your living room. For more information on choosing the right one for your home, read more about rugs on page 161.

Styling Tips for Open Shelving

Styling open shelving areas can be really tricky, and it's important to get it right. No matter what room they are in, they need special attention, since they show up prominently in any marketing photos and are often the focal point in a room.

Here are some dos and don'ts for styling your open shelving:

DON'T

- Don't use your open shelving for storage when staging. When you're staging, use open shelving for styling and making the space appealing.
- Don't leave papers, maps, coil-bound books, notebooks, faded dust jackets, and beat-up paperbacks on these shelves.
- Don't use small accessories and knickknacks. They will make the shelves feel cluttered.
- Don't feel like you need to fill every shelf. It's okay to leave some empty.
- Don't use a lot of dark items on dark shelving; add light and reflective items as well as plants to brighten the shelves.

Before and after photos of shelving in a bathroom.

DO

- Do reduce items to the bare minimum needed to make the shelf look good, and prepack the rest.
- Do strive for balance of weight, texture, and color.
- Do place items that contrast the color of the shelving so that items pop.
- Do fill the largest spaces first, and then go from there.
- Do make use of medium-to-large vases, decorative boxes, sculptural objects, and bowls to fill spaces.
- Do use small- and medium-sized pieces of framed artwork or photography (not personal photos) to lean upright on shelving to fill spaces.
- Do add plants to your shelving.
- Do try arranging items symmetrically for a balanced feeling.
- Do add baskets for warmth and texture.
- Do arrange books visually by color and size, rather than by subject or author.
- Do alternate books lined up side by side with others stacked on top of each other.
- Do try turning books with spines to the wall to create a more uniform color.

Before and after photos of shelving in a dining room.

DINING ROOMS

When staging a dining room, the same principles of reduce and simplify apply. Reduce your furniture to a minimum. If your dining room (or dining area) is small, take out any buffets or large curio cabinets; stage with just a table and six chairs, and possibly a bar cart. If your dining room is medium-sized, you can add a buffet and maybe two more chairs around the table. Don't keep any extra chairs in the corners of the room or serving tables either. The room will look larger and airier if you have less in it. Unless your dining room is very large, definitely don't have any tall cabinets or heavy tall shelving units—they will dwarf the room. Prepack the items that are stored inside the furniture not needed for staging, and put everything in storage till you've sold the house.

Staging Tip!

Stand back and take a photo of your newly arranged shelving—it can help you notice parts that feel crowded or unbalanced. Adjust as needed and take a second photo to compare.

When staging your dining room, remove excess furniture and keep your accessories to a minimum.

Keep your staging accessories simple. Don't set the table for dinner, it looks cluttered. A dining room table can be staged simply with a centerpiece—or with a runner and a centerpiece. Choose a runner in a neutral color contrasting to your table. If your table is dark or medium-toned, choose a white or cream-colored runner. If your table is very light, choose a dark or medium-toned runner to contrast the table. The centerpiece can be a vase of greenery, some candles, or a beautiful bowl.

If you're using a rug under the table for staging, make sure it isn't too small. The chairs should be able to be pulled back and still remain on the rug. Only use staging-friendly rugs (see page 167). But don't feel that it's necessary to have a rug under a dining room table. If you are in doubt as to whether to use the rug you already have, and you have floors that will appeal to your target market, it's better to go without a rug and show your floors.

KITCHENS

Kitchens are critical to a buyer's decision to make an offer. A great kitchen will sell a not-so-great home, and agents will tell you that the condition of the kitchen will make up over 30 percent of the buyer's decision.

If you haven't already read the sections on updating, repairing, decluttering, depersonalizing, and deep cleaning kitchens, go back and read those sections now. Once you're done those things, you've gone a long way toward helping your kitchen's appeal and you're ready to style it. Here are some styling tips:

Kitchen Counters

You want your counters to be almost empty when you show your home. Anything that is left on them should not be left for practical reasons—the practical items that you actually need while you show your home should be stored neatly in your cabinets.

When styling your kitchen, keep your counters clear of your everyday items. Use trays to keep your accessories looking neat and be sure that you tidy your kitchen cabinets—especially any glass-fronted cabinets!

The items left on the counters should be placed to provide texture, color, and contrast, or to connect to buyers emotionally and help them imagine them living an idyllic life in the home. Here are some examples of great staging accessories for your kitchen:

Greenery

All rooms look better with some greenery, and kitchens are no exception. Real plants are ideal, as long as they are healthy-looking and are in proportion to the space, but good fake plants are fine too. Fresh potted herbs and succulents look great on windowsills and open shelving, and they also brighten dark areas under cabinets. See page 172 to learn more about greenery as a prop for home staging.

What's with the Lemons?

Have you ever noticed that many staged kitchens have a bowl of lemons on the counter? Who has a bowl filled entirely with lemons? The reason for this is that all that yellow in one place adds a fantastic pop of bright color! If you have several different types of fruit in one bowl, it looks more cluttered. Also, lemons are healthy, so they fit into an aspirational lifestyle—and they work with any kitchen style or trend.

A Bowl of Fresh Fruit

A classic staging accessory is a bowl filled with either lemons or limes (not both). The simplicity of a single type of fruit adds a solid pop of color that reads great in photos and feels simple and fresh in person. Buyers like to imagine themselves eating healthy foods in their new home, so fruit and vegetables actually make great staging accessories. And of course you can eat them too—just replace them before the bowl gets too empty.

Wood and Wicker

With all the hard and shiny surfaces found in kitchens, they can sometimes feel cold and uninviting. You can counteract this by

adding some warmth with wood accessories and some baskets. Stand some wood cutting boards up in front of your backsplash, alongside a plant. Use a wood bowl or basket for your fruit. Or add some baskets to your open shelving. Another trick that provides warmth is to store whole grains like brown rice and oats in glass jars.

Kitchen Cabinets

The tops of your kitchen cabinets should be completely empty. Baskets, plates, or other decorative items read as clutter when staging and are often distracting in online photos. They also tend to be very taste specific which, of course, doesn't work well in staging. Buyers will look inside your kitchen cabinets, so be sure you have done your decluttering inside them and tidied them up. You want your kitchen to feel like it has ample storage space, so reduce items from crowded cabinets by prepacking.

Kitchen Tables

As I write this, tablecloths are not particularly on trend, so if that's still the case when you're staging your home, don't use one when staging. If your table is rectangular, it can be shown with a runner and a centerpiece. Greenery, flowers, candles, and a bowl or basket of fruit can make effective centerpieces. If your table is round or oval, a centerpiece is all you need.

Staging a Bar Area

It's nice to stage a bar area if you can—something simple to suggest entertaining and relaxing with friends or family. You don't need a lot to do this, just a tray with a bottle of wine and two wine glasses. Or a bottle of champagne in a cooler and some champagne glasses. Sometimes you'll have a little space someplace where a bar area might seem appropriate— maybe on a dining room console table, at the end of a long kitchen counter, or on a deck or patio.

If you already have a bar cart, that's fantastic, but don't load it up with a lot of bottles! Just one is enough, with some glasses and flowers or a plant or other decorative items.

In a family rec space, instead of a bar area, style a refreshment area with some snacks and nonalcoholic beverages.

FAMILY ROOMS, MEDIA ROOMS, MAN CAVES, AND OTHER RECREATIONAL SPACES

While other rooms are often styled luxuriously, these more casual rooms are great places to show buyers the fun they can have living in your home. Most buyers love fun as much as luxury.

In this type of space, it's okay to have a TV as the focal point. But there are lots of other indoor recreational uses that you can suggest to your buyers. And if you have a very large room, it's not a problem to divide the space into separate areas with a different fun activity shown in each. Here are some ideas for your "fun" spaces:

- Games table set up with a game or puzzle
- Adult or children's crafting space or art studio
- Kid's play space
- Piano, drums, guitar, violin, or other musical instrument practice space
- Indoor gym
- Yoga or meditation retreat
- Wood shop
- Large game tables such as billiards, ping pong, or air hockey
- Turntable with vinyl records

As in the living room, the furniture should be reduced and be arranged in a way that invites buyers to walk into the space by not crowding or blocking the buyer's path through the space.

You'll want this space to feel light, bright, and welcoming, just like the rest of the home, so even if it's a media-watching space in a basement, make sure that you have ample lighting. You can also add light-colored throw cushions to dark furniture. And don't forget to include some plants as well!

STAGING OPEN CONCEPT SPACES

Large, open multi-purpose rooms must be broken down into separate areas. Each area must have a separate purpose and be clearly defined. Each must work on its own (both visually and physically), and they must also work together as a whole. Sound complicated? It's not really. Here are some easy guidelines.

How to Define Each Zone

1. *Choose one purpose for each area.* For instance, you might have a kitchen area + a dining area + a casual family TV-watching area. Or a fireplace centered seating area +

a formal dining area. Or a billiard table area + a bar area + a comfortable seating area. Every home is different, but these rules can apply to all homes.

2. *Choose the boundaries for each area and use the furniture and rugs to define these boundaries.* A rug can be used to visually pull the furniture together and can also define the boundaries of the space. Arrange your furniture within the boundaries of the area.

3. *Find the physical center point for each area and center your furniture, and the activity in the area, around it.* A dining space center point may be a hanging pendant light fixture and a table and chairs centered under the fixture. A living space center point might be a coffee table surrounded by comfy furniture. A kitchen center point may be a kitchen island or the sink under a window. A game table will be the center of the gaming area.

4. *Choose a focal point for each area.* This may be the same as the same as the center point or it could be something else. The center point is the actual physical center, whereas the focal point is where your eye is drawn to. For instance, in a comfortable seating area, the focal point might be a fireplace, but the center point might be a coffee table. Be sure the focal point in each area stands out by using contrast, color, scale, and texture (see page 150 for more information on focal points).

5. *Make room between the areas for people to walk easily.* In a small open concept space, keep a minimum of three feet for walkthrough between each area. In a larger space, five feet minimum is preferable.

How to Unify All Zones and Make Them All Work Together

1. *Keep the color palette the same for the whole open space.* Of course neutrals are best for staging, but keep the neutrals the same. And if you have an accent color or two, make sure these colors appear in all of the zones.

2. *Keep the style the same for the whole space.* Whether your style is ultra modern, transitional farmhouse, boho, industrial, or any other style, keep it consistent throughout the whole open space.

OFFICES

Since so many people work from home, a home office can be a really good selling feature. If you don't already have a room in your home designated as an office, try to find a place to stage one in your home.

Before and after photos of office space. This small room felt crowded with two oversized sofas, so for staging purposes, it made sense to show it as an office with a simple desk and chair setup. The room felt a lot larger with less furniture in it, and a home office was a feature that appealed to the buyers.

If you have several bedrooms, it's smart to show one of them as an office. Keep the furniture minimal. A desk, desk chair, a lamp, and maybe a side chair can be enough. If your home is small and you can't set aside a whole room as an office but you have a little nook, set that up with a small desk and lamp. Remember Rule 1 (one purpose for every room) and don't go crowding a desk into a bedroom or living space, but if you have a nook that is separate from the rest of the space, stage it with a small desk.

If you already have an office that you use on a regular basis, be sure you do a lot of decluttering and depersonalizing. Our offices tend to accumulate a lot of papers, cords, and piles of who-knows-what that we no longer use—and that will look messy in marketing photos.

PRIMARY BEDROOMS

Your goal when staging your primary (or master) bedroom is to make it feel calm, relaxing, and high-end—like a private oasis away from the demands of a busy life.

Primary Bedroom Furniture and Accessories

Remember Rule 1 and remove any non-bedroom-specific furniture. Your desk, exercise equipment, storage bins, and any large or unneeded furniture will have to find another home while your house is for sale. The same thing applies to TVs and alarm clocks, since they are a detriment to creating a relaxing sanctuary.

If you have more than one dresser, put the extra dressers in temporary storage and prepack any clothes you won't need for the next few months. If your bedroom is small, it's better if you can manage with no dresser at all. Use a console table instead, since they are narrow and will make your room feel larger.

Staging Tip!

There is no need to be practical when staging. Although you may normally have a dresser or two in your bedroom, it's better to show it with a sitting area or a console table instead—particularly if your bedroom is small. It gives a more spacious and luxurious feeling.

Arrange the furniture so that the head of the bed is on the wall opposite the door to the room. The bed is generally the focal point of a bedroom, and you want to see the focal point as you enter. It's not ideal, but, if you need to, it's okay to put a bed in front of a window, as long as the headboard isn't a high one that blocks a lot of light. You still want the room to feel light and bright. If the layout of your bedroom doesn't allow you to position the bed so you see the headboard as you enter, create a focal point on the wall straight ahead as you enter, possibly with a dresser or console table and artwork.

Symmetry helps a room feel calm and ordered and works especially well in primary bedrooms. So place matching nightstands on either side of the bed and matching lamps on each of the two nightstands. Then hang a mirror or artwork on the wall over the center head of the bed. Arrange the pillows symmetrically on the bed.

Plush rugs feel luxurious and work well in primary bedrooms. Choose accessories that feel expensive and luxurious, such as items that are mirrored or made from metals, natural fibers, wood, or marble. Don't forget to add some greenery or flowers. Hang another piece of artwork over your dresser or console table.

Cool colors, such as soft blues, greens, and lavenders, feel soothing and calming. Jewel tones like amethyst, gold, and emerald feel rich and lush. Either are great choices for this room. And a monochromatic palette of mostly neutrals feels expensive and high-end.

If your bedroom is large enough, set up a cozy reading chair in a corner. Drape a pretty throw on the chair, and add a side table and a reading light next to the chair. Buyers will imagine quiet mornings spent leisurely sipping a coffee and reading a book. But be sure there is ample room surrounding these pieces so that it doesn't feel crowded!

How to Make Your Bed

Have you ever stayed at a hotel where the bedding was white, crisp, and clean? Didn't it feel luxurious and inviting? That's the type of bedding you want in your primary bedroom when staging. White bedding brightens any bedroom and feels clean—and remember, buyers like clean and bright. There is even a style of bedding called hotel bedding which works in any formal bedroom and is a great option for staging. But really, any white cover on a duvet or a white quilt will work. Pillow shams or pillowcases that are exposed should also be white and are often included when you buy a duvet cover or quilt.

White bedding is best for staging, but if the idea of keeping it clean and perfect sounds daunting, store it in your closet or in a bag under your bed and just bring it out for showings.

So how do you make your bed for staging? There are many ways to do it that will look great, but if you're stuck, here is a simple and effective step-by-step formula that will work well in marketing photos and in person for double or queen-size beds.

1. Start by putting the white duvet or quilt neatly on the bed.

2. Take two pillows in white pillowcases and prop them up side by side against a headboard or the wall.

3. Add two more pillows in the shams that came with your quilt or duvet cover and prop them against the first two pillows.

4. In the center of the white pillows, place a dark or brightly colored throw pillow. It should contrast and pop from the white pillows. The contrast will draw buyers' attention to the focal point of the room: the bed.

5. A folded throw added to the foot of the bed is optional.

For a king-size bed, use king-size pillows and shams and a long lumbar throw pillow in the center for contrast.

If you have a platform bed, you might want to tuck in the bedding for a neater look. If you have a bed with a box spring, make sure your box spring is covered. Many people don't have anything covering their box springs, and it makes the bedroom look cheap and unattractive in photos. You can cover yours with either a box spring cover, a white fitted sheet, or a bed skirt.

When you add a new bed skirt, it usually comes out of the package with a lot of wrinkles that show up in the photos. A fast and easy way to get the wrinkles out is to first place the new wrinkly bed skirt on the bed, and then get a spray bottle filled with hot water. Spray the heck out of the bed skirt and then wait for it to dry. Most of the wrinkles will be gone when the bed skirt is dry, but if you have any more, douse the remaining wrinkles and smooth them with your hands. The wrinkles should be gone when the material dries.

Pro Tip!

"Create a soothing sanctuary. The master bedroom is where your buyer will spend one-third of their lives, so why not make sure it looks clean, soothing, and stylish? Add solid white bedding (avoiding busy patterns) and layered pillows while removing excess furniture and clutter. A well-staged master bedroom helps make someone feel like they can move right in."

Anne and Patrick Furlow
Step by Stage Interiors
Lakeland, FL
stepbystageinteriors.com

There are an infinite number of ways to make a bed. Just remember to keep it simple, look for contrast, and if you have any colors in your throw pillows, be sure that they are in keeping with your décor and appeal to buyers.

On Photo Day

Photos pick up on every wrinkle and detail imaginable, so spend a couple extra minutes making your bed *extremely* neatly the day that the marketing photos are taken. It's shocking how many times a well-made bed looks horrible in marketing photos.

Here are two tips to getting it right:

1. Most photos are taken from a lower vantage point than eye level, so after you've finished making your bed, stand back, crouch down, and look at your bed from a lower level so that you have an idea of what the camera might see. You might notice something that you otherwise wouldn't, such as under-bed storage bins peeking out or a sheet hanging at an odd angle.

2. Iron your duvet cover or quilt. But if you're pressed for time or you just don't want to iron it, here is the next best thing: fill a misting bottle with hot water and spray your bed lightly, being sure to hit all the wrinkles. Then wipe the wrinkles flat with a clean hand. When it dries, most of the wrinkles will be gone!

Children's Bedrooms

If your target buyers are families with kids, you will need to stage at least one bedroom as a child's bedroom, if not more. If you have kids yourself, you will be staging with your own children's items. Declutter and tidy their room as much as possible, reduce and simplify their furniture and toys. If your children are sensitive about your upcoming move and don't want their things changed for the staging, don't stress them further. Concentrate your staging efforts on other rooms for the home. But do a thorough tidy before

the photography and encourage them to keep their room neat
and tidy while you are having showings. Make it easy for them by
having some empty bins or bags to throw their things into quickly.

If you don't have any kids yourself, it is a good idea to stage one
or more bedrooms as kids' bedrooms to help your buyers imagine
their family living there. If you already have a twin or double bed
that you can use for this purpose, add neutral bedding and some
children's accessories to make the room more kid friendly.

*Before and after photos of a child's bedroom. The home sellers were using this
room as a home office, but prospective buyers were likely to respond better to a
child's bedroom, so the room was converted to help buyers envision themselves in
the home.*

If you don't have a twin bed to use for this purpose, it's easy to
create a fake bed for staging, and you might be able to do it using
things you already have. Find six or more plastic bins, crates,
or boxes that are about fourteen inches tall. Place a twin bed
skirt that has a fourteen-inch drop on top of the bins. Add an air
mattress (borrow one if you don't have one, or buy one that you
can use for guests in your next home). Cover the mattress with a
duvet, comforter, or quilt—you don't need sheets—and layer several
pillows at the head of the bed. Make it fun and friendly with a cute
stuffed animal, and you have yourself a winning combination. If
you're thinking about doing this to stage your home, speak to your
real estate agent first. Some insist on real beds.

It's easy to create a staging "bed" using things you may already have. This bed was made using four large plastic bins as a base, along with a blow-up mattress, a headboard, and some bed linens.

Money-Saving Tip!

Borrow a couple of toys, kids' books, and artwork from friends or family to help stage your kids' room.

Variation on the above: buy an inexpensive metal portable folding bed frame online to use instead of the boxes and board combination. This is more stable if someone sits on the bed and is preferred by real estate agents for that reason. This bed frame can be used for guests in your next home. I have also created a "bed" by laying two large bookcases on the floor instead of storage bins, and then draping the bed skirt over the bookcases.

Complete your staged children's bedroom with a bedside table with a lamp on top, a desk or play table, a rug, some cute artwork, a few children's books or toys, and possibly additional lighting. Feel free to use more color in a kid's room than you would in the rest of the home.

If you have a very small bedroom in your home, it is especially important to show it with a twin bed so that buyers will be able to instantly see that it is big enough to be used as a bedroom. Without any furniture in the room, it will look even smaller and buyers will question whether the room can fit a bed or not.

BATHROOMS

Primary en suite bathrooms should feel relaxing and spa-like. If you've done Steps One through Five, your bathrooms should already feel more inviting. Here are some styling touches to make them a home run for buyers.

Plants: Every bathroom needs some greenery. Orchids and succulents are great choices for bathrooms. Make sure they are in proportion to the size of your bathroom. If you have a small powder room, place a small succulent on the vanity or a small orchid on the top of the toilet tank. If your bathroom is large, use larger plants, such as a large orchid, for the vanity and a medium-sized succulent on the side of a large spa-like tub. If you have open shelving in your bathroom, that's another great place for a plant.

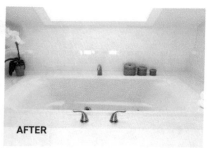

BEFORE

AFTER

Buyers don't want to see your personal items. So put them away while you sell your home and style your bathroom with spa-like accessories.

White towels: Buy some new white towels. White says "clean" to buyers, so add some fresh ones for every bathroom in your home. In addition to hanging them on your towel racks and hooks, you can stack some neatly folded white towels on the side of a tub, roll some in a basket, or fold a hand towel neatly on the side of a sink. But don't use them—they are just for show until your staging is over, then you can enjoy them yourself.

Staging Tip!

Be sure you depersonalize your bathroom and remove any reading material— buyers especially don't want to imagine other people using this room!

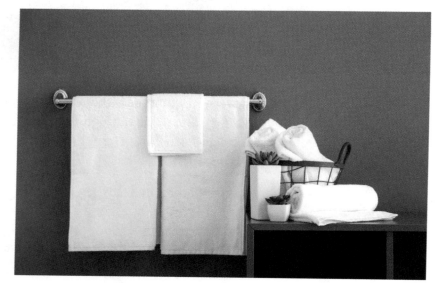

Bath mat: Your bathroom floors should be clear of any bath mats, but a fresh white cotton bath mat folded over the side of the tub works for staging.

Baskets: Add texture and warmth to your bathroom with baskets. They can also add to the spa-like feel. What to put in them? Neatly folded or rolled towels, some high-end bath products, or potted plants, of course.

Candles. Remove any old or half-used candles. Large white pillar candles in a hurricane lamp or oversized white jar candles with high-end-looking labels work best. Place on the side of a tub, on shelving, or on top of a toilet tank.

Shower curtain: Replace a worn, mildewed, or dark shower curtain with a fresh white fabric shower curtain and matching liner.

Soap: Add some fresh, high-end-brand liquid soap for buyers to wash their hands.

LAUNDRY ROOMS

While laundry areas are not key rooms, laundry is a reality for everyone, so make your laundry space more inviting. Finish your Steps One through Five first. Limit cleaning products on open shelving to a bare minimum and place them in a basket. Add a stack of folded white towels, a plant, and maybe a second basket, and you're done. Even a laundry area feels better with a plant and some white folded towels!

GARAGES

When it comes to staging, garages can be more than a place to keep your cars and storage items. They are also a great place to suggest a fun-filled lifestyle to your potential buyers. What sort of fun activities are there to do in your area, and what might buyers be excited about? Kayaks, canoes, motorcycles, skis, snowboards, surfboards, bikes, golf clubs, tennis racquets, and workbenches are all things you could show in your garage that would be appealing to buyers. Put your storage boxes in an off-site storage space and show a few fun things that buyers might want to use in their leisure time instead. Just be sure not to crowd the space and to keep enough room for cars to come and go.

UNFINISHED BASEMENTS, ATTICS, AND STORAGE SPACES

Like the rest of your home, these spaces should look and smell clean, and be well maintained and relatively clutter-free. It's fine to have storage boxes in your storage spaces, but they should look organized and there should be enough room for buyers to get inside and have a good look around to see how big the space is.

If you have an unfinished basement with a concrete floor, give the floor and walls a fresh coat of paint. This can transform the basement into a livable space that feels fresh and a lot more inviting. If it's a dry and usable space, stage as a workshop or kids' play area.

CHILDREN'S PLAY AREAS

If you have kids and are staging their current play area, it can be a little difficult since they probably mess it up on a daily basis. So reduce the number of toys for the time the house is on the market by prepacking whatever they aren't currently playing with, so that they only have a few toys that they really love. A smaller number of toys is easier to maintain and will keep both you and your kids happy. Make cleanup easy with a few bins to throw things into when potential buyers are coming by.

If families with kids are your target buyer, but you don't have children living in your home, find a space to stage as a children's play area to appeal to your buyers. Do you have a space that you're

Staging Tip!

You can't change your square footage, but you can change the amount of perceived usable living space. If you have a space that you're not sure what to do with, or you are using a livable space as a storage space, that would be better shown by converting usable areas in attics, basements, and large stair landings to a kids' play space, an office, or a spare bedroom.

not sure what to do with? Or do you have some livable areas in your home that you are currently using as storage? Add a colorful rug, some kids' furniture, and a few toys to suggest a place where kids can play for your potential buyers.

This was an awkward, unused space at the end of a hallway. By showing it as a children's play area to a target market of families with young children, it gave the space a purpose that would appeal to these buyers.

SUNROOMS, ENCLOSED PORCHES, AND PATIO ROOMS

Sunrooms

Sunrooms are simply rooms in a home that have a lot of windows and are appealing to most buyers, especially in a cool or cold climate. Help your buyer imagine themselves soaking up some sunshine on a cold winter day by staging an inviting room to sip a coffee or read a book. You can use comfy furniture meant for indoor living, like sofas and chairs on the lighter side, whether in color or actual weight. Or, since this is a space where you can bring the outdoors in, indoor/outdoor lounge furniture can work too. Look for furniture made from teak (or other woods), wicker, or wrought iron—all accessorized with a hefty amount of comfy cushions. Natural-fiber rugs work well in these spaces, and be sure to use plenty of plants!

Enclosed Porches

Enclosed porches at the front of a home often become a free-for-all-storage space and are invariably used to pile coats, footwear, and everything including the kitchen sink. Since it will be the first room that buyers see—even before they get inside the actual front door— use this space to make a great first impression. Turn your enclosed porch into an inviting bonus space by removing any storage items, and greet your buyers with a welcoming and comfortable space to come home to and relax in. Stage yours with on-trend indoor/outdoor furniture and rugs, lots of plants and flowers, and a refreshment tray.

This enclosed porch was the first room buyers would see, so it made sense to turn it into an inviting space that they would fall in love with before they even entered the home.

Patio Room

In warm-weather climates, a patio room can be a great selling feature and is often a key room of the home. Be sure that yours feels relaxing and luxurious—the ideal place to get together with family or entertain guests. The furniture should be indoor/outdoor lounge furniture or high-end patio furniture. Lavish the space with lots of plants and flowers to "bring the outside in." If you have a pool in your patio room, be sure it is clean and well maintained. Add a floating lounger to entice your potential buyers and place a tray with a pitcher and glasses on a table to suggest refreshments.

Staging the Exterior of Your Home

The "Six Steps to Successful Staging" not only apply to the interior of your home, but must also be applied to the exterior of your home to achieve maximum curb appeal. In the previous chapters there are recommendations for exterior repairs, updates, depersonalizing, and decluttering that are essential to getting top dollar for your home. So be sure you review these recommendations and follow through with the ones that are necessary for your home.

Step One. Repair: page 57

Step Two. Update: page 89

Step Three. Depersonalize: page 106

Step Four. Declutter: page 127

Step Five. Deep Clean: page 141

This section will help you with the last step in staging your home and how to specifically stage and style the exterior of your home. It is important to stage the exterior so that your house leaves buyers with a positive and welcoming first impression.

Let's start with the "The Essential Rules of Staging—That Have Nothing to Do with Design," outlined in Step Six of this book, and talk about how they apply to your home's exterior.

Rule One: One Purpose for Each Room

Think of your outdoor spaces as separate "rooms" that have distinct purposes. The outdoor spaces in your home may include areas such as a front yard, a porch, a patio, a deck, a courtyard, a pool area, a children's play area, a hot tub, or a just plain open space.

List the spaces outside your home and give each space a single purpose. For instance, if your patio is currently used as a combination eating area, kid's play space, exercise space, and workshop, choose just one purpose for that space and remove the things that don't apply to that specific activity.

Rule Two: The Purpose of Each Room Should Be the One Originally Intended.

When this rule is applied to the exterior of the home, it refers to the permanent outdoor structures. Think about what the original intention of that space might have been. If it was designed with a specific activity in mind, then it will be an easy fit to show that space used for that purpose.

Now create a plan for your outdoor spaces. For example, in a home that has the following outdoor spaces, here is a sample plan that lists the purpose for each space and how to stage it.

Front Lawn

Purpose: to showcase home and increase curb appeal.
Plan: stage with fresh shrubs, flowers, planters, and mulch.

Front Porch

Purpose: to relax and talk with neighbors and family.
Plan: stage with a porch swing, rocking chairs, and a refreshment tray with a pitcher and glasses on the side table.

Back Deck off the Kitchen

Purpose: dinners with family and friends.
Plan: stage with a BBQ, outdoor table and chairs, umbrella, flowers and herbs in containers, string lights, and candles in hurricane lamps on the table.

Staging Tip!

Use an edger or shovel to sharpen the edge between the grass and the shrub border. It instantly makes an outdoor space look neat and well maintained.

Even if there is no room between your front door and the street, you can still add "curb appeal" with attractive container plants.

Patio

Purpose: outdoor lounge area.
Plan: stage with attractive outdoor lounge furniture, throw pillows, string lights, outdoor rug, planters, and a tray containing wine bottle and wine glasses.

Back Lawn

Purpose: fun play area.
Plan: stage with outdoor ping pong table or kids' play structure.

Sunny Side Yard

Purpose: vegetable garden.
Plan: stage with raised beds.

Obviously, it makes sense to use things that you already own or can borrow when you are staging. If you were already using a sunny side yard for growing vegetables, then leaving your existing raised beds there shows buyers a potential use for that space.

Money-Saving Tip!

If you are planning to put your home on the market in the spring, a cost-effective way to add a pop of color is to plant a bag of bulbs the previous fall. Your home will be ready for potential buyers when you're ready to put it on the market.

Choose a fun, relaxing, or useful activity to present in each outdoor space. Other ideas you might want to consider:

- A hammock: to suggest relaxation.
- Lawn games: badminton, soccer, horseshoes, croquet, boules, and bocce are just a few games that could be set up on a large lawn.
- Fire pit with seating.
- Water features such as bird baths and fountains.

By showing an appealing purpose for all potential areas in your exterior, you help the buyer connect emotionally to your home by getting them excited about all of the fun activities they could be doing if they lived there. And you also increase your home's perceived value by showing your outdoor space as usable square footage on top of your home's interior square footage.

Rule Three: Highlight Selling Features

First, make sure that buyers can actually see your home. This might sound obvious, but I've been to so many homes that have such large overgrown foundation bushes or trees that are too big for the space that the home is either largely or completely obscured. It is impossible to get a good photo of the outside of your home if it can't be seen! Often these bushes or trees haven't been maintained, are scraggly, and are not appealing anyway, so remove them and plant smaller, healthier shrubs. Also, don't let your windows be obstructed by large overgrown bushes or trees. You want to let all the light possible into the house. Trim or remove where necessary.

Think about your home's exterior selling features and be sure that they stand out by removing anything that obstructs them from the buyer's view. Make your exterior selling features very obvious and spend time staging them. For example, if your home has a nice screened-in gazebo, clean it up, paint it, and show it with nice outdoor furniture, an outdoor rug, and some on-trend accessories. Or, if you have a gorgeous perennial garden, be sure it is weeded

Staging Tip!

Try to create a natural "flow" from one area of your yard to another. If your yard is on a slope, install some levelled paving stones to make it easier for potential buyers to walk around.

Staging Tip!

Hate weeding or pressed for time? Just weed along the path to the house and around the front door. That's the most important area.

and that buyers have an unobstructed view of it as they come into the yard. If you're selling off-season and your garden isn't looking its best, try to include some great photos of the garden with your online marketing photos. Determine your home's exterior selling features and plan what you will do to make them stand out.

Rule Four: Make Each "Room" Appear as Large as Possible

Make each outdoor space appear as large as possible by trimming any large bushes that are taking over patios or play areas. Limit the amount of furniture in each space—don't overcrowd. Select just enough furniture to show how the space can be used and remove the rest.

Rule Five: Make Each "Room" Appear as Light as Possible

This rule can be applied outdoors as well. Outdoor lights can be beautiful, so string some around your patio, deck, or balcony. If your patio feels dark due to heavy trees overhead, trim them. Depending on the style of the property, if you have a lot of trees in front of your home, they may be creating a lot of heavy shade and feel unwelcoming.

Rule Six: Do Not Obstruct the Buyers' Flow as They Walk through the Space

Place outdoor furniture in a way that welcomes buyers into the space. Don't put things in the buyer's path. Put container plants in places where they can be seen but aren't in the way. If you have a lounger sitting in the way of some stairs, move it or remove it. Move the BBQ grill if it blocks the buyer's view of the flower bed as they come out of the home. Trim large branches and bushes that obstruct doors, steps, and pathways.

CURB APPEAL DESIGN AND STYLING

In order to best improve your curb appeal, go stand at the curb (or wherever buyers will first see your home) and stop. Have a really good look. Pay attention to both the overall look and first impression—as well as to the details. Then walk slowly toward the front door. Stop a couple of times along the way. Make note of any things you think can be improved. Here some specific things to look for.

The Focal Point

Just like a room, the front of your home needs a focal point. The focal point in curb appeal is usually the front door of the home. Your front door should stand out from the rest of the home and invite the buyer in. Front doors are often painted a different color from the rest of the home for a reason: it makes the door stand out and draws your eye toward it, thereby creating a focal point. If you're not sure about the color of your front door, I recommend getting a paint color consultation. The color you choose needs to work with the rest of your home's exterior materials and colors and can be difficult to get right.

Another way to draw attention to the front door is with flowers in planters. Bright pops of colorful flowers invite buyers to come forward and welcome them to the home. Lighting around your front door brings attention to that area at night.

Color Palette

All colors that can be seen from the curb must work together: the colors of the exterior walls of your home, the roof, the foundation, all visible structural features, the front door, even the walkway to the home. If you didn't read the tips on choosing the right colors for your home, you can go back and see them on page 89.

Pro Tip!

"If your home is on a busy road, plant evergreens, mixed shrubs, or tall grasses to provide a barrier between your home and the road. Try to make it as naturalistic as possible rather than planting everything in a straight row—this will make the screening less obvious."

*Claire Cornish
Hudson Planting
Irvington, NY*

For this staging, the color yellow is repeated in the front door, the cushions on the porch swing, and the flowers in the flower bed.

But if you have already done any needed paint updates, now is the time to add additional color through furniture or accessories at the front of the home, as well as any plantings. Choose one or two colors to repeat—possibly on the front door, some cushions on the outdoor furniture, and with some flowers planted near the front door. Or you can go with a neutral palette outside by using neutral colors and lots of greenery. Just be sure that you have some contrast to draw your eye to your focal point.

Staging Tip!

View the back of your home's exterior through the windows where the buyers will most likely get their first view and through the main entrance to the back yard.

More Outdoor Staging Tips

MULCH

I highly recommend adding fresh mulch before you list your house. It will make a huge improvement in your curb appeal. But I have a personal pet peeve about mulch, so here it is: so many people use mulch that isn't the right color. The color of the mulch used should be very similar to the color of the soil found in that geographic location. If the soil color in your area is brown, please don't use red mulch! It looks very unnatural! Find some dark brown mulch, please. If the soil color in your area is red, go ahead, then red mulch will look great. Sandy-colored soil areas look great with light brown/beige-y mulch. Having said that, fresh mulch is a fantastic idea. It makes a huge improvement in your curb appeal and doesn't cost that much in relation to its positive impact.

CLIMATE

Climates vary widely around the world, so do what makes sense for your location and use elements that are found naturally in that area. If you're in a dry or desert environment, pebbles, stones, cactus, ornamental grasses, succulents, crushed stone, or gravel are great options.

BALCONIES AND SMALL PATIOS

Outdoor space is a fantastic selling feature when selling an apartment or townhouse-style home. Maximize yours so that it feels like an extra room in your home and increases your perceived square footage.

Here are some tips to help you make yours look great:

- Use small-scale furniture.
- Use an outdoor rug to spruce up unattractive balcony floors.
- Add plants: try container plants in a corner, along a railing, or on a table and hanging plants.
- Be sure not to crowd the space.

Summary

- Determine your focal point and style your room around it. If your focal point is one of your home's selling features, buyers will be sure to notice it.

- Consider the contrast and balance of texture and color in each room.

- Stand just outside each room and look at it with a critical eye. This will be where buyers create their first impression of that room, so it's the most important vantage point.

- The Six Essential Rules of Staging will help you style for staging, and you don't have to be a designer to make them work!

- Reduce your furniture and choose light, neutral pieces where possible.

- Be sure that your artwork is staging-friendly, and don't hang it too high! In most cases, the center of the artwork should be approximately fifty-eight inches above the floor, i.e. eye level.

- Adding a healthy (or good fake) plant to every room makes your home more inviting.

- The Six Essential Rules of Staging work for styling your front and backyard as well as the interior of your home.

Living in Your Home While It's on the Market

It can be difficult to live in your home while it's for sale. After all, you're trying to present an idealized lifestyle to prospective buyers while, at the same time, living a real life with all of its challenges.

So how do you maintain your home's pristine staged condition while you're living in it? And how do you leave your home in a way that ensures successful showings—some of which may be at the last minute?

There are several things you can do during this time to make life easier for yourself and keep your home looking showing-ready.

Staging Tip!

Staging your home is not a reason to overprice it. It's true that staging will help your home appeal to buyers, but you still need to keep your home's listing price competitive with others in your market. The longer your home sits on the market, the more likely it is that your final selling price will drop. Most well-priced, well-staged homes get multiple offers shortly after listing.

Valuables and Privacy

If your home is staged beautifully and priced right, you should have a lot of buyers coming and going through your doors—especially shortly after you first go on the market. So before your home is listed, be sure that you've secured any valuables you own. You can store them outside your home with a trusted friend or family member or in a safety deposit. Or keep them inside your home in a locked cabinet or safe.

Think about your privacy and remove or store any documents containing financial and personal information. Turn off desktop computers when you leave and take laptops and tablets with you.

Also, prescription drugs should be either kept in a locked cabinet or taken with you when you leave for showings.

Pets

If you have pets, you'll need to have a pet plan in place before you have any showings. Where will your pets be during showings and where will you put their food, toys, bedding, cages, etc.?

Dogs: Dogs should be removed during showings. Take your dog on a hike, a doggie play date, or to a kennel. Hide dog beds, crates, food, toys, and other dog-related items.

Cats: If possible, take your cats out of the house with you in carriers. This can be very difficult to do with some cats. Fortunately, cats are fantastic at hiding, so if your cat is difficult to crate and your home is odor-free, buyers may not know it is there. Keep the litter box in an unobtrusive spot and be sure it's super clean before you leave the home.

Reptiles, amphibians, birds, rodents, and small mammals: Find a temporary home for these animals while you are selling your home. These animals can put off some buyers and their terrariums and cages can be smelly.

Fish: Fish tanks can be difficult to move, so just make sure that yours is clean and well maintained.

Staging Tip!

Keep pet food in airtight containers to help keep your home smelling fresh.

Keeping Your Home Clean and Clutter-free

Don't undo the hard work you've done deep cleaning your home. The most effective way to maintain a clean and clutter-free home is to establish a daily routine, so that your home is neat and tidy by the end of each day and it never becomes overwhelming, and a weekly routine that focuses on tasks that need a little less attention. By putting a simple system in place, you don't have to go into panic mode every time you have a viewing. Here is a daily and weekly routine for you to consider that will keep your home show ready.

DAILY ROUTINE

- Make your beds when you wake up.
- Tidy your kitchen after each meal and leave the kitchen clean at the end of the day.
- Keep cleaning supplies in each bathroom and do a one-minute mini-clean every day.
- Set a timer for ten minutes of decluttering each day.
- Put toys away at the end of the day.
- Scoop cat litter twice daily.

WEEKLY ROUTINE

- Dust and vacuum high-traffic areas inside the home several times a week and low-traffic areas once a week.
- Clean kitchen top to bottom. If you've left it clean at the end of each day, there shouldn't be much to do.
- Clean bathrooms. If you're doing a daily mini-clean, this won't take long.
- Check for odors.
- Empty cat litter and clean tray at least twice a week.
- Maintain your curb appeal: tidy porch and front of home, clean around front door, mow lawn, weed in key areas, rake or blow leaves.

Pro Tip!

"Connect with your buyers and have them fall in love with your home by appealing to all their senses. Sight: stage to create a 'welcome home' feeling. Smell: incorporate fresh scents. Taste: tantalize the taste buds by putting out cupcakes or cookies in the kitchen. Hearing: play soft music. Touch: use different-textured furnishings like fur, feather, silk."

Anwesha Banerjee
East West Interiors
Sammamish,
Washington
www.eastwestinteriors.us

Create a chore chart for each family member. If you don't normally have a professional cleaner, you might want to schedule one for a weekly cleaning while you're on the market—but even if you do this, it is important to keep up the daily routine yourselves.

There are several systems already established for maintaining a clean, clutter-free home. My personal favorite is the Fly Lady System, so a lot of my suggestions originate from this system. If you're curious about it, there are several blogs and great channels on YouTube that explain how it works.

Have a Go Bag Ready

When you leave your home for a showing, you'll want to take some things with you. Make a list of what they might be, for instance: laptops and tablets, prescriptions, mail, pet items, and that big pile of paper sitting on the kitchen counter. Have a bag or plastic bin designated to put these things in as you walk out the door. Keep your list in the go bag so that you always know where it is and you will avoid any last-minute panics.

Last-Minute Prep Before Showings

You've got a showing in an hour. What do you need to do so that your home feels inviting to prospective buyers? Remember that you want your home looking light, bright, clean, and clutter-free. Make yourself a personal checklist so that you don't forget anything. Here are some things you may want to include:

- Set thermostat to a comfortable temperature.
- Open all blinds and curtains to their fullest.
- Turn on all lights.

- Light a fire in the fireplace.
- Play soft music.
- Fluff pillows and fold throws.
- Put away remote controls.
- Put away toys and other things left out.
- Stow away kitchen counter items, wipe down counter, empty trash.
- Stow away bathroom toiletries and garbage can, lower toilet lid, and tidy towels.
- Stow pet food, litter box, and other pet items.
- Hide outdoor trash cans and check tidiness of front of home for curb appeal.
- Pack your go bag and leave!

Buyer Feedback

After a showing, most buying agents will give some feedback about what the prospective buyer thought about your listing. Every buyer is looking for something different, so your home won't be for everyone. They might say your house is too small or too big for the buyers that came through. Or maybe there were things that buyers just didn't like. Be grateful for the feedback, even if it is negative. Listen to the comments—and if there is something that you can do to alleviate an issue, do it quickly so that future buyers don't have the same experience.

Conclusion

My goal was to guide you through the home staging process and to provide useful tips and tricks along the way. If you found this book helpful, please let me know—I would love your feedback. What tips did you actually use? Which sections did you most benefit from? If you have tips that I didn't include, share them! Others may find them useful.

Blog: secretsofhomestaging.com

Instagram: secretsofhomestaging

Facebook: secretsofhomestaging

Email: secretsofhomestaging@gmail.com

Since this book will be distributed all over the world, I have made an attempt to include images from homes in many locations. But terms for the rooms and furniture within our homes—and the selling process itself—differ everywhere. With that in mind, here are some of the words that I have used and some alternate terms that you may find more familiar.

Foyer—entrance, front hall

Living room—sitting room, lounge, front room, receiving room, reception room, salon, drawing room, parlor

Family room—den, game room, rec room, television room, media room, rumpus room, play room

Primary bedroom—master bedroom

Bathroom—washroom, toilet, WC, restroom, lavatory

Powder room—two-piece bathroom, half-bathroom, loo

Laundry room—utility room

Sofa—couch, chesterfield, divan, settee, davenport

Buffet—sideboard, hutch

Cabinets—cupboards

Closet—cupboard, built-in wardrobe

Patio room—Florida room, lanai, solarium, garden room, sun parlor, conservatory

Backyard—back garden, garden, terrace, yard, grounds, lawn

Real estate agent—estate agent, agent, REALTOR®, real estate broker, broker

I apologize for any that I've left out, and I hope the advice in this book works for you regardless. Best of luck in the sale of your home—and wherever life takes you after you've sold!

Acknowledgements

As a visual-thinking art school graduate who hadn't written anything longer than a thousand words before, I can't believe I've finished an entire book. It took me about a year, but I did it, along with staging and selling my own home!

Of course I didn't do it on my own. I'm very fortunate to have friends and family who happen to have relevant communication skills and were kind enough to volunteer them in service of my manuscript or book cover design, along with heavy doses of encouragement: my partner Sean Moore, my parents Marilyn and Jim Prince, and my good friends Cate Harty, Gisèle D'Amour, Claire Cornish, sut Fitterman, and Jennifer Adams. Thank you too to Bill Ford-Sussman for getting me started in the home staging business, my children, Louis and Maya, for helping with it, and to Heather Bancroft for making it way more fun.

To Chris McKenney and Yaddyra Peralta at Mango Publishing: thank you for taking this book on and for responding to my many requests and questions along the way. To the home stagers who contributed Pro Tips features for this book—and Audra Slinkey and Cass Aarssen who provided glowing endorsements—I am grateful for your time and your contributions.

Lastly, thank you to the home sellers and real estate agents that I have had the privilege of working with and who trusted me with their homes and their listings. I loved working with you all (well, almost all) and I learned a lot along the way. I hope that by writing this book, the skills and knowledge that I gained during that time will go on to help other people.

About the Author

Karen Prince is an award-winning certified home stager who brings her unique design and marketing experience to the art of home staging. After a successful career both as an art director at top creative agencies and a designer in illustrated book publishing, she transitioned to home interiors—quickly becoming one of the most sought-after home stagers in New York.

Mango Publishing, established in 2014, publishes an eclectic list of books by diverse authors—both new and established voices—on topics ranging from business, personal growth, women's empowerment, LGBTQ studies, health, and spirituality to history, popular culture, time management, decluttering, lifestyle, mental wellness, aging, and sustainable living. We were recently named 2019 *and* 2020's #1 fastest growing independent publisher by *Publishers Weekly.* Our success is driven by our main goal, which is to publish high-quality books that will entertain readers as well as make a positive difference in their lives.

Our readers are our most important resource; we value your input, suggestions, and ideas. We'd love to hear from you—after all, we are publishing books for you!

Please stay in touch with us and follow us at:

Facebook: Mango Publishing
Twitter: @MangoPublishing
Instagram: @MangoPublishing
LinkedIn: Mango Publishing
Pinterest: Mango Publishing
Newsletter: mangopublishinggroup.com/newsletter

Join us on Mango's journey to reinvent publishing, one book at a time.